www.osha.gov

> **Occupational Safety and Health Act of 1970**
> "To assure safe and healthful working conditions for working men and women; by authorizing enforcement of the standards developed under the Act; by assisting and encouraging the States in their efforts to assure safe and healthful working conditions; by providing for research, information, education, and training in the field of occupational safety and health."

This publication provides a general overview of a particular standards-related topic. This publication does not alter or determine compliance responsibilities which are set forth in OSHA standards and the *Occupational Safety and Health Act*. Moreover, because interpretations and enforcement policy may change over time, for additional guidance on OSHA compliance requirements, the reader should consult current administrative interpretations and decisions by the Occupational Safety and Health Review Commission and the courts.

This document is intended to provide relevant information to employers and employees in determining whether respirators are needed, and, if so, how the respirators should be selected and used. This publication does not replace the official Respiratory Protection standard (29 CFR 1910.134).

Material contained in this publication is in the public domain and may be reproduced, fully or partially, without permission. Source credit is requested but not required.

This information will be made available to sensory-impaired individuals upon request. Voice phone: (202) 693-1999; teletypewriter (TTY) number: 1-877-889-5627.

Small Entity Compliance Guide
for the
Respiratory Protection Standard

Occupational Safety and Health Administration
U.S. Department of Labor

OSHA 3384-09
2011

U.S. Department of Labor
Hilda L. Solis, Secretary of Labor

Original cover illustrations created by Attiliis & Associates

Contents

**Occupational Safety and
Health Administration**

Agencies are required to prepare and publish one or more guides to assist small entities in complying with regulations for which an agency is required to prepare a final regulatory flexibility analysis. (Requirement is in the *Small Business Regulatory Enforcement Fairness Act*, (P.L. 104-121, March 29, 1996, as amended by P.L.110-128, May 25, 2007).

**Occupational Safety and
Health Administration**

Introduction

Agencies are required to prepare and publish one or more guides to assist small entities in complying with regulations for which an agency is required to prepare a regulatory flexibility analysis. *(See the Small Business Regulatory Enforcement Fairness Act, (P.L. 104-121, March 29, 1996, as amended by the P.L. 110-128, May 25, 2007).)*

This Small Entity Compliance Guide (SECG) is intended to help small businesses comply with the Occupational Safety and Health Administration's (OSHA) Respiratory Protection standard (63 FR 1152; January 8, 1998). While the guide is for small entities, the guide itself is not small. OSHA's goal for this document is to provide small entities with a comprehensive step-by-step guide complete with checklists and commonly asked questions that will aid both employees and employers in small businesses with a better understanding of OSHA's respiratory protection standard. The reader should be advised that OSHA also has other shorter documents and visual aids that may be used to better understand respiratory protection and the OSHA standard itself. That information can be found on OSHA's website at www.osha.gov.

If the employees of a small business are only exposed to nuisance dusts and relatively non-toxic chemicals and use only a few types of relatively simple respirators, knowledge of the guide and materials supplied by the respirator manufacturer may be sufficient for the small business owner or an employee to become qualified as a program administrator. If more dangerous chemicals or high exposures are present, or sophisticated respirators are used, the program administrator must have more knowledge or experience. In these circumstances, it may be necessary for the administrator to seek out the expertise needed or to obtain appropriate training.

OSHA's original Respiratory Protection standard was adopted in 1971 from an existing American National Standards Institute (ANSI) standard. On October 5, 1998, OSHA issued a revised standard that updated and replaced that 1971 standard. At that time, in 1998, OSHA reserved the definition under *(d) (respirator selection)* for the *Assigned Protection Factors (APFs)*, and *Maximum Use Concentrations (MUCs)* and *Table I: Assigned Protection Factors* values until further rulemaking was completed.

In addition, the revised 1998 Respiratory Protection standard included a new provision that allowed the development of new fit tests. In compliance with this provision, OSHA approved and adopted an additional quantitative fit testing protocol, the controlled negative pressure (CNP) REDON fit testing protocol, in 2004. *(See Appendix A of the standard.)*

In August 2006, OSHA again revised the standard by adding definitions for APF and MUC and a table (Table I) of APF values. This guide provides a discussion of these APF provisions and their role in the overall Respiratory Protection standard.

History of OSHA's Respiratory Protection Standard

Year	Event
1971	The existing American National Standards Institute (ANSI) standard adopted as OSHA's Respiratory Protection standard
1998	OSHA's Final Revised Respiratory Protection Standard (Assigned Protection Factors reserved)
2004	CNP REDON Fit Test Approved for Use
2006	Final *Assigned Protection Factors Rulemaking (APF)* including APFs, MUCs, Table I: Assigned Protection Factors (71 Fed. Reg. 50122)

OSHA's Respiratory Protection standard specifies only the minimum requirements for an effective respiratory protection program. Under the standard, OSHA may require you to establish a respiratory protection program when exposure to an airborne contaminant or to low oxygen levels can cause illness or injury to an employee and when these health effects can be prevented by the use of adequate engineering and administrative controls and/or the appropriate selection and use of a respirator. OSHA may also require you to establish a respiratory protection program while these engineering and administrative controls are being installed or maintained and repaired, or for emergencies. You are encouraged to exceed these minimum criteria if doing so enhances the safety and health of your employees. This SECG provides a sample respirator program to guide small business administrators. *(See Attachment 4 of this guide.)*

This document is advisory in nature, informational in content, and is intended to assist employers by using plain English to explain each provision of the standard, whenever possible. However, technical terms that apply to respiratory protection have legal definitions, as set forth in the Respiratory Protection standard. In this guide, whenever these terms are used, they are used only as they are legally defined. A list of these terms can be found under *(b)(definitions)* of the Respiratory Protection standard. A copy of the standard is included in this guide under Attachment 3.

The Respiratory Protection standard (29 CFR 1910.134) establishes, in one place, the required program for properly selecting and using respirators. All mandatory respirator use is covered by the Respiratory Protection standard. The Respiratory

Protection standard also applies to: Shipyards (29 CFR 1915.154); Marine Terminals (29 CFR 1917.92); Longshoring (29 CFR 1918.102); and, Construction (29 CFR 1926.103). The final standard covers required respiratory protection for use against hazardous airborne workplace exposures, including biological hazards.

The audience for this guide

You should read this guide if it is likely that you will need to establish and implement a respiratory protection program for your business. This guide is intended to assist program administrators, employers who need to develop a program, employees who may be required to wear respirators, and licensed medical professionals who must evaluate an employee's ability to wear respirators, among others.

Program administrators need to develop a written respiratory protection program that covers procedures for the use of respirators in any work area in which employees are exposed to airborne hazards. This guide provides information on procedures that will help the administrator develop a program for the particular workplace. The program needs to cover each provision of the standard. All required elements of the respiratory protection program must be in writing unless a particular element does not apply to your workplace. For example, if no employees volunteer to wear respirators, then the program administrator does not need to develop procedures for that type of respirator use. Employees themselves will find useful information in this guide on training and medical examinations. Licensed healthcare providers will find additional information in this guide on the timing of medical examinations and follow-up exams for employees who use respirators, as well as information about the types of respirators that are available.

This document provides guidance only, and does not alter or determine compliance responsibilities, which are set forth in the *Occupational Safety and Health (OSH) Act (29 U.S.C. 655)*. The guide does not replace the official *Respiratory Protection standard (29 CFR 1910.134)*. A copy of the Respiratory Protection standard is provided in Attachment 3 of this guide. You must refer to the standard to ensure compliance. Lists of appendices for this guide and for the Respiratory Program standard are provided under "How to use this guide."

There are two limitations to the use of this guide. First, interpretations and enforcement policy may change over time. To stay up-to-date on interpretations and enforcement policies, you should consult current administrative interpretations and decisions by the Occupational Safety and Health Review Commission and the courts for additional guidance on OSHA compliance requirements. And second, new fit tests may be approved through Section 6(b)(7) rulemaking.

In 27 states and territories, occupational respiratory requirements are enforced by the state agency responsible for the OSHA-approved State Plan. These states are: Alaska, Arizona, California, Hawaii, Indiana, Iowa, Kentucky, Maryland, Michigan, Minnesota, Nevada, New Mexico, North Carolina, Oregon, Puerto Rico, South Carolina, Tennessee, Utah, Vermont, Virginia, Washington, and Wyoming. Connecticut, Illinois, New Jersey, New York, and the Virgin Islands operate OSHA-approved State Plans that apply to state and local government employees only.

State Plan states are required to adopt and enforce respiratory protection standards that are either identical to or at least as effective as the Federal OSHA standards. These states are also required to extend the coverage of their respiratory protection standard to state and local government employees, including paid, and in some states, volunteer firefighters who are otherwise not covered by the Federal standard. The information in this guide should be equally applicable to you if you are located in a State Plan state, although you should check to see if there are any unique or additional requirements that may apply.

How to use this guide

This guide is divided into the same sections that appear in the final Respiratory Protection standard. *(See Attachment 3.)* The organization of the guide follows the same organization as the corresponding provision of the standard, proceeding from paragraph (a)(Permissible Practice) to mandatory appendices of the Respiratory Protection standard (§ 1910.134.) A special feature of the electronic version of this guide on OSHA's webpage is included in the Table of Contents. This feature allows you to "click" on the section of interest to you in the Table of Contents and go directly to that portion of the guide.

References to the appendices to the Respiratory Protection standard are in italics in the text of this guide.

§ 1910.134 Respiratory Protection Standard
Section (a) – Permissible Practice
Section (b) – Definitions
Section (c) – Respiratory Protection Program
Section (d) – Respirator Selection
Table I: Assigned Protection Factors
Table II: Oxygen Deficient Atmospheres
Section (e) – Medical Evaluation
Section (f) – Fit Testing
Section (g) – Use of Respirators
Section (h) – Maintenance and Care of Respirators
Section (i) – Breathing Air Quality and Use
Section (j) – Identification of Filters, Cartridges
*   and Canisters*

Section (k) – Training and Information
Section (l) – Program Evaluation
Section (m) – Recordkeeping
Section (n) – Effective dates
Section (o) – Appendices

The appendices to the Respiratory Protection standard are:

Appendix A to § 1910.134: Fit Testing Procedures (Mandatory)
  Part I. OSHA-Accepted Fit Test Protocols
    Table A-1: CNP REDON Quantitative Fit Testing Protocol
  Part II. New Fit Test Protocols
Appendix B-1 to § 1910.134: User Seal Check Procedures (Mandatory)
Appendix B-2 to § 1910.134: Respirator Cleaning Procedures (Mandatory)
Appendix C to § 1910.134: OSHA Respirator Medical Evaluation Questionnaire (Mandatory)
  Part A. Section 1. (Mandatory)
  Part A. Section 2. (Mandatory)
Appendix D to § 1910.134: Information for Employees Using Respirators When Not Required Under the Standard (Mandatory)

The attachments in this guide are:
Attachment 1 – the glossary and list of definitions from the Assigned Protection Factor rule
Attachment 2 – a complete set of the checklists used in this guide
Attachment 3 – a copy of the Respiratory Protection standard
Attachment 4 – a Sample Program
Attachment 5 – NIOSH MultiVapor Information
Attachment 6 – NIOSH tables of cartridges and canisters by APFs (modified to OSHA's APFs)

Citations to the standard provided in each section enable you to compare the text in this guide with the standard. *(See Attachment 3 of this guide for a copy of the Respiratory Protection standard.)* For example, to review the new assigned protection factors and maximum use concentrations in the final standard, at *(d)(3)(ii)(A)-(B)*, it might be useful to know that you will need to begin with *section (d)* and proceed through *(d)(1)* and *(d)(2)* to *(d)(3)* and then through *(d)(3)(i)* to *(d)(3)(ii),* and so forth.

Citation for Assigned Protection Factors and Maximum Use Concentrations, under *paragraph (d) Selection of Respirators*

Citation to the standard	Name of Section in Standard	Small Entity Compliance Guide
Paragraph *(d)(1)-(2)*	*Respirator Selection*	Employers need to know specific information on: NIOSH certification, unknown exposures; workplace factors; user factors, the two major types of respirators; respirators for oxygen deficient, and other IDLH atmospheres. *Table II: Oxygen Deficient Atmospheres,* is described in (d)(2).
Paragraph *(d)(3)-(d)(3)(i)*	*Respirators for non-IDLH atmospheres*	When providing respirators, employers must provide respirators that are adequate to protect employee health and ensure compliance with all other OSHA requirements under routine and reasonably foreseeable emergency situations.
Paragraph *(d)(3)(i)(A)*	*Respirators for IDLH atmospheres* *(A) Assigned Protection Factors (APFs)* Employers must use the assigned protection factors listed in Table I to select a respirator that meets or exceeds the required level of employee protection.	Employers need to know specific instructions on how to select respirators using *Table I. Assigned Protection Factors.* *Table I. Assigned Protection Factors* is described in this paragraph.
Paragraph *(d)(3)(i)(B)*	*Respirators for IDLH atmospheres* *Maximum Use Concentrations (MUCs)*	The employee's exposure must be at or below the MUC when the exposure is measured outside the respirator. Instructions on how to select respirators using MUCs, including the limitations of MUCs, are provided.
Paragraph *(d)(3)(ii)-(iv)*	Respirator selection for chemical and physical form of contaminant, and other provisions.	

In the final Respiratory Protection standard, *Table I: Assigned Protection Factors* is at the end of section *(d)(3)(iv)*. From this example, it is clear that major provisions, such as those covering APFs and MUCs, are actually subparagraphs of the larger selection citation provision for non-IDLH hazards. It is these citations to the standard that are included in the text of this guide, as appropriate.

Respiratory protection equipment

Respirators are devices that protect employees from inhaling harmful substances, including chemical, biological, and radiological agents. These substances can be in the form of airborne vapors, gases, dust, fogs, fumes, mists, smokes, or sprays. Some respirators also ensure that employees do not breathe air that contains dangerously low levels of oxygen or that is otherwise immediately dangerous to life or health (IDLH), (e.g., life-threatening exposures during interior structural firefighting.) Respirators may be used to provide protection during routine operations where engineering controls and work practices are not able to provide sufficient protection from these hazards, or in emergencies.

In situations in which employees are exposed to harmful airborne hazards, respirators must "seal off" and isolate the user's respiratory system from the contaminated environment. The risk that a user will experience an adverse health outcome when relying on respiratory protection is a function of the toxicity or hazardous nature of the air contaminants present, the concentrations of the contaminants in the air, the duration of exposure, and the degree of isolation provided by the respirator. When respirators fail or do not provide the degree of protection expected by the user, the user is placed at an increased risk of any adverse health effects that are associated with exposure to the respiratory hazards present. Furthermore, the margin for error in IDLH atmospheres is slight or nonexistent because an equipment malfunction or employee mistake can, without warning, expose the employee to an atmosphere incapable of supporting human life. Such exposure may disable the employee and require an immediate rescue if the employee's life is to be saved. Therefore, it is critical that respirators are properly selected and used in compliance with the Respiratory Protection standard (29 CFR 1910.134).

Respirators provide protection from respiratory hazards only when they are properly selected and used in compliance with the *Respiratory Protection standard (29 CFR 1910.134 and 29 CFR 1926.103)*. The final Respiratory Protection standard applies to general industry, construction, longshoring, shipyard, and marine terminal workplaces. A copy of the standard is provided in Attachment 3.

Atmosphere-supplying respirators are used to provide breathing air from a source independent of the ambient atmosphere. Respirators that supply breathing air are generally used in highly hazardous work environments. It is critical that such respirator systems provide breathing air of optimal quality and that the equipment operates reliably.

The two types of such equipment are:

- Self-contained breathing apparatus (SCBA) units, for which air is supplied from a tank (a cylinder of compressed air or oxygen). For this type of respirator, the source of the breathing air is designed to be transported by or with the equipment user.

- Supplied-air respirators (SARs) (also known as air-line respirators), which receive air from a connecting hose. The source of air is either a pressurized cylinder or an air compressor. Because the employee does not carry the air on his or her back when using a SAR, breathing air can be provided over a longer time period than is the case with an SCBA.

Examples of atmosphere-supplying respirators with tight-fitting facepieces and positive pressure characteristics include:

Self-contained breathing apparatus (SCBA), supplied-air respirator (SAR) and full elastomeric facepiece;

Abrasive-blasting SAR in the continuous mode and full elastomeric facepiece; and

Supplied-air respirator (SAR) with an escape bottle and full elastomeric facepiece.

Pressure-demand respirators are positive pressure atmosphere-supplying respirators that admit breathing air to the facepiece when the positive pressure is reduced inside the facepiece by inhalation.

An air-purifying respirator (APR) is a respirator which removes contaminants from the air. An atmosphere-supplying respirator, or Supplied-air respirator (SAR), is one which provides clean breathing air from an uncontaminated source.

Elastomeric facepieces include facepieces made from Natural or Synthetic Rubber (e.g., EPDM); EPDM is an acronym for a specific type of rubber; that is, Ethylene propylene diene M-class rubber.

Examples of an air-purifying respirator and an atmosphere-supplying respirator

Air-purifying respirators (APR) remove contaminants from the air

Half mask filtering facepiece
Dust Mask

Supplied-air respirators (SAR) or Atmosphere-supplying respirators provide clean air from an uncontaminated source

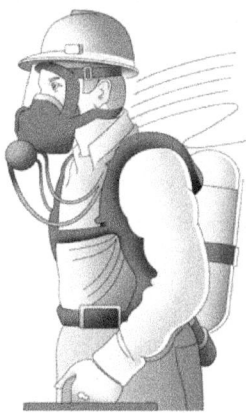

Self-contained Breathing Apparatus
(SCBA) Full facepiece Elastomeric

OSHA's Respiratory Protection Standard

The Respiratory Protection standard requires employers to establish and maintain a respiratory protection program to protect their respirator-wearing employees. OSHA revised the original 1971 Respiratory Protection standard in 1998. The new standard incorporates scientific principles and technologies that emerged since 1971. Because of advances in technology, many areas covered by the previous standard had become outdated.

The final revision of the Respiratory Protection standard is intended to:

- Enhance the protection of employee health.

- Promote more effective use of respirators.

- Make it easier for you to comply with its provisions.

- Make it easier to understand the policy and procedures you must follow when implementing a respiratory protection program.

- Supersede most respiratory provisions in existing standard.

The Respiratory Protection Program

A respiratory protection program is a cohesive collection of written worksite-specific procedures and policies that, taken together, address all respiratory protection elements required by the standard. For example, a respiratory protection program must contain specific procedures describing how respirators will be selected, fitted, used, maintained and inspected in a particular workplace. Section (c) of this guide contains more information on respiratory protection programs.

When respirators are used during operations where exposures exceed OSHA's permissible exposure limit (PEL), use of properly functioning respirators is essential to ensure that employees are not placed at significant risk of material impairment of health. Respiratory protection is necessary in situations where engineering and administrative controls are insufficient to reduce airborne hazards, in emergencies, in situations in which engineering and other controls are being installed or maintained, in oxygen deficient atmospheres, or for internal structural firefighting. The final Respiratory Protection standard establishes the minimum elements of a comprehensive program that are necessary to ensure effective performance of a respirator.

When to use the Respiratory Protection Program

Generally, you are required to establish a respiratory protection program whenever you or OSHA requires your employees to wear respirators. For example, you may need to establish a respiratory protection program:

- If your employees work in situations where the level of oxygen is insufficient or potentially insufficient.

- If your employees are potentially exposed to harmful levels of hazardous gases or vapors.

- If your employees are exposed to other potential respiratory hazards, such as dust, airborne biological hazards, mists, fumes, sprays, and other airborne particles.

You need to supply employees with respirators when all preferred methods of protecting them from breathing contaminated air have been determined to be insufficient to reduce the contamination to non-hazardous levels. You must also consider the potential for emergencies, that is, for reasonably foreseeable emergencies, when evaluating the respiratory hazards in the workplace. These preferred methods include:

- Engineering controls, such as: local or general dilution ventilation, change of the work process, isolation or enclosure, or substitution, and

- Administrative controls, such as: employee rotation, or scheduling major maintenance for weekends or times when few employees are present.

If you have any questions about when to supply your employees with respirators, refer to the copy of the standard in Attachment 3.

Updates to OSHA's Respiratory Protection Standard

In the final Assigned Protection Factor rule, OSHA revised its existing Respiratory Protection standard to add definitions and requirements for Assigned Protection Factors (APFs) and Maximum Use Concentrations (MUCs). The revisions also supersede the respirator selection provisions of existing substance-specific standards with these new APFs (except for the respirator selection provisions of the 1, 3-Butadiene Standard). As part of the final Assigned Protection Factor rule, pertinent provisions of the substance-specific standards that were superseded were modified in each individual substance-specific standard to make clear where the Respiratory Protection standard is to be followed, thereby reducing any confusion when referring to those substance-specific standards.

The Agency developed the final APFs after thoroughly reviewing the available literature, including chamber simulation studies and workplace protection factor studies, comments submitted to the record, and hearing testimony. The final APFs provide employers with critical information to use when selecting respirators for employees exposed to atmospheric contaminants found in general industry, construction, shipyards, longshoring, and marine terminal workplaces. Proper respirator selection using APFs is an important component of an effective respiratory protection program. Accordingly, OSHA concludes that the final APFs are necessary to protect employees who must use respirators to protect them from airborne contaminants.

Major new provisions and other non-mandatory changes included in the final standard.

The Respiratory Protection standard has been updated and now includes the following important new provision:

- Assigned Protection Factors (APFs), Maximum Use Concentrations (MUCs), and APF Table I.

    And other changes:

- New fit test procedures – Controlled Negative Pressure REDON (CNP REDON)

Assigned Protection Factors (APFs) and Maximum Use Concentrations (MUCs)

OSHA published the final Respiratory Protection standard in January 1998, and reserved the APF provisions, (i.e., the APF and MUC definitions and the Table of APFs) (63 FR 1203). The rulemaking on the reserved APFs of the Respiratory Protection standard was completed on August 24, 2006 (71 FR 50122). The rule amends *29 CFR 1910.134(d)(3)(i)(A)* and *(d)(3)(i)(B)* of the Respiratory Protection standard by specifying a set of APFs for each class of respirators. The new provisions for APFs, MUCs, and Table I cover selection procedures for respiratory protection. These procedures are discussed in more detail in the following section on respirator selection. The APFs specify the highest multiple of a contaminant's permissible exposure limit (PEL) at which an employee can use a respirator.

New Fit Test Procedures - Controlled Negative Pressure REDON (CNP REDON)

The 1998 revised Respiratory Protection standard allowed the development of new fit tests. This provision is contained in *Part II of Appendix A of the standard*. A copy of the Respiratory Protection standard is provided in this guide under Attachment 3. This provision for new fit test procedures specified, in part, the procedure individuals must follow to submit new fit testing protocols for the Agency's consideration. In compliance with this provision, OSHA has approved and has adopted an additional quantitative fit testing protocol, the controlled negative pressure (CNP) REDON fit testing protocol, for inclusion in *Appendix A of the Respiratory Protection standard. (69 FR 46986) (See Section (f) of this guide.)*

The benefits of the Respiratory Protection Standard

The updated standard now provides:

- A complete set of definitions that will eliminate confusion about terminology and how these terms

OSHA®
Occupational Safety and
Health Administration

apply to respirators and their use. *(See: Attachment 1 of this guide (APF Glossary of Definitions); and the definitions under Section (b) of the standard).*

- Criteria for selecting respirators. *(See Section (d) of this guide.)*
- *General information*
- *Assigned Protection Factors*
- *Table I: Assigned Protection Factors*
- *Maximum Use Concentrations*

When issuing the 1998 rule, OSHA estimated that compliance with the standard would prevent hundreds of deaths and thousands of illnesses in U.S. workplaces each year (63 FR 1173). The APFs in the final rulemaking help ensure that these benefits are achieved, as well as provide an additional degree of protection. These new APFs reduce employee exposures in some instances to several Section (6)(b)(5) chemicals covered by standards with outdated APF criteria, thereby reducing exposures to chemicals such as asbestos, lead, cotton dust, and arsenic. While the Agency did not quantify these benefits, it estimated that thousands of employees would have a higher degree of respiratory protection under this APF standard. The Respiratory Protection standard has been determined to be economically and technologically feasible for covered industries.

In addition to health benefits, OSHA believes that other benefits result from the harmonization of APF specifications, thereby making compliance with the respirator rule easier for employers. Employers no longer have to consult several sources and several OSHA standards to determine the best choice of respirator, but can make their choices based on a single, easily found regulation. In addition to having only one set of numbers (i.e., APFs) to assist them with respirator selection for nearly all substances, some employers may be able to streamline their respirator stock by using one respirator class to meet their respirator needs instead of several respirator classes. The increased ease of compliance also yields additional health benefits to employees using respirators.

The revised APFs clarify when employers can safely place employees in respirators that impose less stress on the cardiovascular system (e.g., filtering facepiece respirators). Many of these alternative respirators may have the additional benefit of being less expensive to purchase and operate. OSHA estimated that over 15,000 employees used respirators that fall into this group (i.e., employees that may safely shift to a less expensive respirator).

Points of Contact for additional information

For additional assistance in establishing and implementing a respiratory protection program, contact the OSHA area office nearest you. If you are unable to contact your local OSHA area office, you may contact the appropriate OSHA regional office for information or assistance. A list of OSHA regional offices is at page 118.

Section (a): Permissible practice

When engineering controls are not feasible, or while engineering controls are being put in place, appropriate respirators must be used.

(a)(1) Engineering controls

To prevent illness or diseases caused by breathing hazardous air in the workplace, you must use engineering controls to the extent feasible to prevent contamination of the workplace atmosphere. When engineering controls are not feasible, or while engineering controls are being put in place, appropriate respirators must be used.

How to know if the atmosphere in your workplace is hazardous

An atmosphere is hazardous if it does not contain sufficient oxygen, or if it contains chemical, biological, or radiological contaminants in sufficient quantity to harm the health of employees. Section (d) of this guide contains information on how to identify and evaluate respiratory hazards in your workplace.

What are engineering and administrative controls?

Engineering controls physically change the work environment to reduce employee exposure to air contaminants. Such engineering controls may include:

- Change of the work process
- Isolation or enclosure of the work process or of employees
- Local exhaust or general dilution ventilation
- Substitution of less hazardous substances for harmful materials

Administrative controls involve changes in the length of time or the time of day in which an employee can be exposed. Examples of administrative controls are:

- Employee rotation
- Rescheduling work in area to times when air contaminant levels are low

What guidance is available on the type of engineering and administrative controls that may need to be put in place?

Potential sources for this type of information include:

- Trade associations.

- Manufacturers or suppliers of materials or equipment associated with the creation of air contaminants.

- Your workers' compensation insurance carrier.

- OSHA Consultation Program (See http://www.osha. gov/dcsp/smallbusiness/consult.html) for the list of:

    - states with consultation programs

    - industrial hygiene consultants.

(a)(2) Providing employees with respirators

You must provide respirators when such equipment is necessary to protect the health of employees. The respirator provided must be suitable for its intended purpose. When you are required to provide respirators, you must establish and maintain a respiratory protection program.

The requirements for a respiratory protection program are described in Section (c) of this guide.

How do I know if the Respiratory Protection standard applies to me?

You should use the information collected through the steps covered in *paragraph (a)(1)* to determine whether the Respiratory Protection standard applies to you. For example, information on the type and levels of hazardous airborne exposures in your workplace and on the engineering and administrative controls available to you should be used when evaluating the need for a respirator program.

The vendor who supplies your engineering controls may be able to help you determine whether the controls will adequately protect your employees from respiratory hazards. You must evaluate the level of contamination in your workplace after the engineering controls are installed, as explained in Section (d) of this guide.

How do I know what type of respirator is suitable for protecting the employees' health?

Proper selection of respiratory protection equipment involves the evaluation of the workplace environment, types of job functions that are performed in the workplace, identification of reasonably foreseeable emergencies, employee health conditions, and unique facial characteristics that may affect proper use. Section (d) of this guide provides further information about selecting a suitable respirator.

CHECKLIST FOR PERMISSIBLE PRACTICE

√ Check all that apply:

Hazard Determination

Is there a hazardous atmosphere in your workplace, which has (check all that apply):

❏ Insufficient oxygen

❏ Harmful levels of chemical, biological, or radiological contaminants

❏ Known and reasonably foreseeable emergencies related to...

❏ Unknown exposure levels or exposures to substances without an OSHA PEL

If you did not check any of the boxes above, the Respiratory Protection standard **does not** apply to your workplace.

If you checked any of the boxes above, the Respiratory Protection standard **may** apply to your workplace.

OSHA requires use of the following methods to control the hazardous atmosphere(s) in your workplace:

❏ Engineering controls, such as ventilation, isolation or enclosure of the work process, or substitution of non-hazardous materials for the materials that pose respiratory hazards; and

❏ Administrative controls, such as worker rotation, or scheduling major maintenance for weekends or times when few workers are present.

When engineering controls are not feasible, or while engineering controls are being installed or maintained, or whenever there is an emergency, appropriate respirators **must** be used.

Does your workplace have (check the box to indicate yes, and check all that apply):

❏ Sufficient engineering controls to prevent illness or diseases caused by breathing hazardous air in the workplace

❏ Sufficient administrative controls to prevent illness

If you did not check **both** of the boxes above, the Respiratory Protection standard **does apply** to your workplace, and you must develop a written respiratory protection program that is specific to your workplace.

Occupational Safety and Health Administration

Is employee rotation acceptable as an interim administrative control while engineering control measures are being developed and implemented?

Rotation is an acceptable practice for less-toxic contaminants. It is never permitted for protection against cancer-causing substances. In addition, many of OSHA's substance-specific health standards contain ceiling limits that may limit the use of employee rotation. If respirators are also necessary to protect the health of the employee while engineering controls are being developed, they must be provided.

Section (b): Definitions

This section of the Respiratory Protection standard contains definitions of terms used in the text of the standard. The definitions clarify the requirements of the standard. The definitions from the final Respiratory Protection standard (63 FR 1152; January 8, 1998), and from the final Assigned Protection Factors standard (71 FR 50122; August 24, 2006), have been combined under Attachment 1 to facilitate ease of use.

The terms are contained in *paragraph (b)* of the standard. The full text of the final *Respiratory Protection standard (63 FR 1152)*, with the new definitions and Table of APF values *(Assigned Protection Factors standard), 71 FR 50122*, is provided in Attachment 3.

As OSHA developed this Small Entity Compliance Guide, the sections were written using the terms from the standard. As you review this document, if you have any questions about a term that is used, you should review the definition of the term in Attachment 1 to clarify exactly what is being discussed. The terms Permissible Exposure Limit (PEL) and Employee Exposure are both defined (see Attachment 1 of this guide.) PELs are OSHA's enforceable exposure limit values and should not be confused with threshold limit/exposure limit values (TLVs) or recommended exposure limits (RELs). These and other terms from the APF standard can be found in Attachment 1 of this guide.

Section (c): Respiratory protection program

Whenever respirator use is required by the employer or by OSHA, this section of the Respiratory Protection standard dictates that the employer must:

- Develop a written respiratory protection program with procedures that are specific to your worksite;

- Implement the program and update it as necessary; and

- Assign a qualified program administrator to run and evaluate the program.

Additionally, you are required to ensure that certain requirements of the respiratory protection program are followed by employees who wear a respirator voluntarily (that is, they wear respirators even though respirator use is not required by either you or OSHA).

(c)(1) Program development and implementation

You are required to develop and implement a written respiratory protection program and to update it as necessary.

Program Development

You must develop a written respiratory protection program that includes procedures for the use of respirators in any work area where protection from airborne hazards is required. The procedures in your program must be specific to your particular workplace. All required elements of the respiratory protection program must be in writing.

Why a written program?

The program must be in writing because health and safety programs are usually more effectively implemented and evaluated if the procedures are available in a written form for study and review. Also, a written respiratory protection program is the best way to ensure that the unique characteristics of the worksite are taken into account. Developing the written program encourages you to thoroughly assess and document information pertaining to respiratory hazards posed to your employees both during normal operating conditions and during reasonably foreseeable emergencies.

Program Content

You are required to include procedures for the following elements (as applicable) in your respiratory protection program:

- Selecting appropriate respirators for use in the workplace.

- Training employees in the proper use of respirators (including putting them on and removing them), the limitations on their use, and their maintenance.

- Providing medical evaluation of employees who must use respirators.

- Fit testing tight-fitting respirators.

- Using respirators properly in routine situations as well as in reasonably foreseeable emergencies.

- Ensuring adequate air supply, quantity, and flow of breathing air for atmosphere-supplying respirators.

- Establishing and adhering to schedules for cleaning, disinfecting, storing, inspecting, repairing, removing from service or discarding, and otherwise maintaining respirators.

- Regularly evaluating the effectiveness of the program.

The checklist in this section on establishing a written respiratory protection program at page 16 provides a quick list to use for guidance on the required content of the respiratory protection program.

Program Implementation and Updating

Once you have established a written program that covers all the required elements that apply to your workplace, you then must ensure that the program is appropriately implemented. Implementation of the program must be administered and overseen by your program administrator.

Once your program has been implemented you must ensure that it is updated *as necessary* to reflect relevant changes in the workplace. That is, you need to revise the elements of the program that have been affected by changes that relate to respiratory hazards in work areas. For example, you need to revise the appropriate sections of your written program if new processes or new chemicals are introduced into the workplace that could impact respirator use.

In addition, if you make any changes in the types of respirators used or in any of the other elements of the respiratory protection program, you must make appropriate revisions to the written program and ensure that they are implemented.

(c)(2) Where respirator use is not required

Voluntary use is when an employee chooses to wear a respirator even though the use of a respirator is not required by either you or by an OSHA standard.

What is meant by voluntary use of respirator equipment?

Where respirator use is not required, you must ensure that all employees who use a respirator voluntarily are provided with certain basic information on proper respirator use. Additionally, you must ensure that employees are included in your program provisions for medical evaluations, and for cleaning, storage, and maintenance of respirators, as applicable.

Providing basic information to voluntary respirator users

You may allow an employee to use a respirator voluntarily if you determine that the respirator itself will not present: a hazard to the employee due to misuse; other hazards or conditions in the workplace; or a hazard to an individual employee, based on medical conditions. In such cases, you may provide employees with respirators or allow them to use their own respiratory protection. *(See (c)(2) of the standard.)* If you allow such use of a respirator, you must provide the voluntary

respirator user with the advisory information in *Appendix D* of the standard. This appendix provides basic information on the proper use of respirators for employees who are voluntary users of the equipment and thus are not required to undergo training. These precautions can be presented to the employee either verbally or in a written form. *(See section (k) of this guide on Training and information.)*

Applicable components of the respiratory protection program

You must ensure that the following elements of your respiratory protection program are implemented for voluntary respirator users:

(i) If filtering facepieces are the only respirator being worn voluntarily, you are only required to provide the employee with a copy of *Appendix D* and make sure that the respirator itself is not creating a hazard, such as dermatitis from a dirty respirator.

(ii) Elements of the program that apply to voluntary users (using respirators other than filtering facepieces (i.e., dust masks) involve:

- Provisions for medical evaluation of employees.
- Establishing and adhering to schedules for cleaning, disinfecting, storing, inspecting, repairing, removing from service or discarding, and otherwise maintaining respirators.

Implementation of the elements of the program for a voluntary respirator user will ensure that the respirator is used properly and does not create a hazard to the user.

- A dirty respirator could cause dermatitis.
- A dirty or poorly disinfected respirator could cause an unnecessary inhalation hazard.
- A respirator wearer's health could be jeopardized due to an undetected medical condition (e.g., asthma, heart condition.)

What types of respirators do the voluntary use requirements apply to?

This requirement applies primarily to tight-fitting negative pressure APRs, but would also apply to powered APRs if an employee elected to voluntarily use this type of respirator.

Do I need to have a written respiratory protection program if only voluntary users wear respirators at my facility?

No, if the only respirators being worn voluntarily are filtering facepieces (dust masks).

Yes, if other respirators, such as elastomeric APRs or powered APRs, are being used voluntarily. In this case,

your written program needs to include only the elements that pertain to voluntary users, e.g., a section on medical evaluations, and one on inspection, care, and maintenance.

When employees choose to voluntarily use respirators in the workplace, you must provide the employee with a copy of the mandatory document found in *Appendix D* of the standard.

Who is responsible for any costs associated with voluntary use of a respirator?

You are not required to pay for filtering facepiece respirators used voluntarily by employees.

If the employer determines that any voluntary respirator use is permissible, the employer must provide the respirator users with the information contained in *Appendix D of the standard ("Information for Employees Using Respirators When Not Required Under the Standard.")*

If you permit the use of respirators other than filtering facepieces, you must pay for required medical evaluations for voluntary users and provide voluntary users with appropriate facilities and time to clean, disinfect, maintain, and store respirators.

(c)(3) Program administrator

You must designate a program administrator to run the program and evaluate its effectiveness.

An individual is qualified to be a program administrator if he or she has appropriate training or experience in accord with the program's level of complexity. This training or experience is appropriate if it enables the program administrator to fulfill the minimum requirements of recognizing, evaluating, and controlling the hazards in your workplace. For example, if your program requires air-supplying respirators for use in immediately dangerous to life or health (IDLH) environments, your program administrator must have training and experience pertaining to the use of this type of equipment. Similarly, if you do not use air-supplying respirators and do not have significant respiratory hazards at your workplace, someone with less experience or training might be able to effectively serve in this position.

Ultimately, the appropriate qualifications for your program administrator must be determined based on the particular respiratory hazards that exist, or that are reasonably anticipated, at your workplace.

How do I, or a designated employee, become a qualified program administrator?

If your workers are exposed only to nuisance dusts and relatively low-toxicity materials, and they use only a few types of relatively simple respirators, knowledge of this guide and materials supplied by the manufacturer may be sufficient for you, or a designated employee, to serve as the program administrator.

If more dangerous substances are present, if the potential for high exposures exists, or if more complex respirators are used, the program administrator must have more extensive experience and/or training. In these circumstances, you may need to seek out the expertise needed or obtain appropriate training.

Is there a list of approved training courses my program administrator can attend?

No, OSHA does not provide a training course specifically to train respiratory protection program administrators, nor does OSHA require program administrators to attend a specified course. OSHA only requires the program administrator to have an adequate level of training or experience to deal with the complexity of the respiratory protection program at the worksite.

You may want to check with trade associations or adult education programs run by universities or technical and vocational schools in your area. The OSHA Consultation Program can help you identify appropriate training courses, or, if you hire a consultant to help you with your respiratory protection program, he or she may be able to provide training.

How will OSHA determine that a person is experienced and/or trained to be a respiratory protection program administrator?

Usually, the OSHA compliance officer will review the written program and interview the respiratory protection program administrator. Questions asked during the interview are likely to focus on determining how familiar the program administrator is with the OSHA Respiratory Protection standard and the use and application of the respirators at the particular workplace. Significant deficiencies in the written program also could indicate a lack of training and understanding of the standard.

Only one person can fulfill the primary responsibilities of running the program, unless your company has more than one worksite. In that case, you may have a program administrator for each site. Ordinarily, however, you cannot divide the responsibilities among several employees. Requiring an administrator with sole responsibility helps ensure the integrity of the program by maintaining continuous oversight from one person. Nonetheless, the administrator may rely on other employees to help run parts of the respiratory protection program (e.g., fit testing, medical evaluations).

One of the program administrator's primary responsibilities is to evaluate the program. Although OSHA recognizes the value of an objective assessment, the Agency did not want to burden small businesses with the cost of arranging for an outside party to conduct the evaluations, and the standard, therefore, allows program administrators to perform the program evaluations required under the standard.

(c)(4) Employer-provided respirators

You must provide respirators, training, and medical evaluations at no cost to employees who are required to wear a respirator for protection from respiratory hazards at your workplace. This requirement reflects the philosophy that employers are obligated to provide and pay for necessary personal protective equipment (such as respirators) used by employees on the job.

Section (d): Respirator selection

This paragraph requires the employer to evaluate respiratory hazard(s) in the workplace, identify relevant workplace and user factors, and base respirator selection on these factors. The paragraph also specifies respirators for use in IDLH atmospheres, and limits the selection and use of air-purifying respirators.

(d)(1)(i) General guidelines for selection

You must base selections of respirators on the hazards to which your employees are exposed and must consider how workplace and user factors affect respirator performance and reliability.

What are workplace and user factors?

Workplace factors refer to the actual workplace facility and its geographic characteristics, among other factors. User factors refer to the distinguishing characteristics of the individual employee. Some examples include the following:

- The level of the contaminant in relation to the APF of available respirators

- The conditions of the workplace (e.g., size, configuration, temperature, humidity) of the workspace

  - Are employees equipped with atmosphere-supplying respirators able to fit into any tight space in your workplace?

  - Would the temperature and humidity affect the effectiveness of filters, cartridges, and other respirator parts, as well as the comfort of the wearer?

- Ease of employee communication

  - Are your employees wearing respirators able to communicate with one another and warn one another of hazards?

- Ease or difficulty of the work or rate of activity

  - Are your employees doing heavy lifting that may deplete the air supply of a self-contained breathing apparatus (SCBA)?

  - Would a fast work pace lead to discomfort, causing the employee to move the respirator and, thus, affect the protection afforded by the respirator?

- The type of workplace tasks and proximity to the source of contamination (e.g., cutting wood on a band saw would differ from hand polishing a wood veneer on furniture.)

  - Would hospital emergency medical staff be close to infectious clients?

- The location and movement of other personnel and equipment
  - Would the mobility of your employees or the presence of moving machinery entangle the airlines of atmosphere-supplying respirators?

(d)(1)(ii) Selected respirator must be certified by the National Institute for Occupational Safety and Health (NIOSH)

All respirators must be certified by NIOSH and used in compliance with the conditions of certification.

(d)(1)(iii) Employers need to identify and evaluate worksite hazards

- Identify the respiratory hazards to which your employees are exposed and evaluate these hazards.
- Determine the state and physical form of the respiratory hazard.
  - Are they solids, liquids, or gases?
  - Are they particulate, radioactive or chemical substances?
- Estimate or measure employee exposures to the hazards.
- Assume IDLH atmospheres if unable to estimate an employee's exposure.

Potential Respiratory Hazards:

Listed below are potential respiratory hazards:

Dusts and fibers are solid particles dispersed into the workplace atmosphere through mechanical processes such as crushing, grinding, drilling, abrading, blasting, shaking or physiological processes such as coughing, sneezing. Examples include: silica, metal dust in baghouses, and asbestos. Once an employee's hands and garments, boots, and respirators are contaminated with lead or asbestos, other employees can also be exposed just by handling, or shaking, the contaminated equipment.

Biological hazards include living organisms such as bacteria (e.g., Legionella pneumophila which causes Legionnaires' Disease), viruses (e.g., coronavirus which causes severe acute respiratory syndrome [SARS]), fungi, and other organisms, as well as dead organisms or parts of organisms. Examples of the latter include ground parts of plants (e.g., flour) and parts of animals (e.g., dead skin cells/dander).

Fumes are solid particles that are formed when a metal or other solid vaporizes and the molecules condense (or solidify) in cool air. Examples are metal fumes from smelting or welding. Fumes also may be formed from processes such as plastic injection or extrusion molding.

Mists are tiny droplets of liquid suspended in the air. Oil mists can be produced from lubricants used in metal-cutting operations, acid mists from electroplating, and paint-spray mist from spraying operations.

Gases are materials that exist as individual molecules in the air at room temperature. Examples are welding gases, such as acetylene and nitrogen, and carbon monoxide produced from internal combustion engines.

Vapors are the gaseous form of substances that are normally in the solid or liquid state at room temperature and pressure. They are formed by evaporation. Most solvents produce vapors. Examples include toluene and methylene chloride.

Suggestions for Measuring or Making "Reasonable" Estimates of Employee Exposures

- Personal monitoring is the most accurate way of obtaining employee exposure information. Sampling equipment and analytical methods are available for substances regulated by OSHA's Air Contaminants standard (29 CFR 1910.1000 and 29 CFR 1926.55). OSHA has specific monitoring requirements for its substance-specific standards (e.g., benzene or asbestos). See subpart Z of 29 CFR parts 1910 and 1926, for OSHA's substance-specific standards.

- If there is no specific monitoring requirement, you can also estimate exposures by monitoring fixed locations or by sampling for short time periods. If you do this, you should measure under worst-case conditions to be sure that you are providing adequate protection for your employees. For example, even though employees generally move about and do not spend most of their work shift near the source of emissions, if you select a respirator based on a reading obtained from a fixed sample collected close to the source of the emission, the respirator selected is more likely to provide adequate employee protection. Similarly, although process emissions under non-peak conditions will obviously be less than at peak conditions, a respirator selected on the basis of a reading obtained from a spot sample taken when the emissions are highest (when the process is operating at peak conditions) is more likely to provide sufficient protection.

- Data may be available from previous exposure measurements. For example, studies may have been conducted in your industry. Your trade association may have data, or manufacturers of products or materials used in your workplace may have conducted laboratory tests that provide employee exposure data. To generalize from data obtained from these sources or an industry-wide survey, however, you must show that the conditions that existed in the survey, such as the processes, types of materials, control methods, work practices, and environmental conditions, are similar to those in your own workplace.

- You should be aware that exposures can be quite variable from day to day and from employee to employee. It is, therefore, important always to err on the side of over- rather than under-protection.

- You may wish to consult with health and safety professionals in evaluating exposures. However, consultation is not mandatory. The respiratory protection program administrator should have the necessary qualifications. You can often obtain assistance through the OSHA Consultation Program. A list of Consultation Programs is included under Attachment 2. An additional source of assistance might be your insurance carrier.

- You may be able to demonstrate, through information on processes and reasonable assumptions about potential maximum use concentrations (MUCs), that IDLH conditions would not occur. Under such a scenario, after a thorough review of relevant information, you may be able to place values on the unknown exposures. That is, you may be able to reduce, delineate, or eliminate the unknown exposures. After review of all available material, you need to make reasonable assumptions and develop conservative estimates. The material you used and the assumptions and findings you relied upon in place of a measurement of an employee's exposures should be in your written program. If new materials and sources of information are generated or conditions or processes or types of materials used in your processes change, or if new cases of airborne illness occur, you need to review and possibly update your written program.

If you do not know your employees' exposure levels

You must consider the worksite atmosphere Immediately Dangerous to Life or Health, (IDLH), and select respirators on that basis. IDLH means an atmosphere that poses an immediate threat to life, would cause irreversible adverse health effects, or would impair an individual's ability to escape from a dangerous atmosphere *(29 CFR 1910.134, paragraph d)*.

(d)(1)(iv) You must provide a sufficient number of respirators to correctly fit the user

A sufficient number of respirator models and sizes must be available to employees so that they can find the respirator that is acceptable to, and correctly fits, them.

(d)(2) Respirators for IDLH atmospheres

(d)(2)(i) Types of respirators

Atmospheres that are immediately dangerous to life or health (IDLH) require the highest level of respiratory protection and reliability. You must provide either of the following for use in IDLH environments:

- Full-facepiece pressure-demand SCBAs that are certified by NIOSH for a minimum service life of 30 minutes.

- Combination full-facepiece pressure-demand supplied-air respirators with auxiliary self-contained air supply.

(d)(2)(ii) Respirators for escape from IDLH atmospheres must be NIOSH-certified for escape from the atmosphere in which they will be used

For example, for formaldehyde exposures, escape respirators may be full-facepiece with chin style, front, or back-mounted industrial-size canister approved for protection against formaldehyde (29 CFR 1910.1048 at: *http://www.osha.gov/pls/oshaweb/owadisp.show_ document?p_table=STANDARDS&p_id=10075*).

(d)(2)(iii) You must consider all oxygen deficient atmospheres to be IDLH

Atmosphere-supplying respirators must be used in oxygen deficient atmospheres (where oxygen is less than 19.5%). Employers must provide employees with full-facepiece pressure demand SCBAs or combination full-facepiece pressure demand supplied-air respirators with auxiliary self-contained air supply. There is an exception that applies to well-controlled atmospheres, where the reason for the oxygen levels being reduced below 19.5% is known and the reduced oxygen level is stable and not changing. (You may use any atmosphere-supplying respirator if you can demonstrate that, under all reasonably foreseeable conditions, the oxygen concentration in the work area can be maintained within the ranges specified in *Table II of 29 CFR 1910.134*.) *(See also Table II.)*

Work operations being conducted in well-controlled atmospheres where oxygen levels are deficient (below 19.5 percent) are typically permit-required confined spaces. *(See OSHA's Permit-Required Confined Space standard, 29 CFR 1910.146 at: http://www.osha.gov/ pls/oshaweb/owadisp.show_document?p_table= STANDARDS&p_id=9797.)*

(d)(3) Respirators for non-IDLH atmospheres

(d)(3)(i) You must provide respirators that are adequate to protect employee health and ensure

compliance with all other OSHA requirements under routine and reasonably foreseeable emergency situations

The General Duty Clause of the OSH Act requires you to protect your employees from all hazardous substances, even those not regulated by OSHA. Consult the Material Safety Data Sheet (MSDS) sent by your supplier if you have questions about the toxicity of a particular substance. For further assistance in ascertaining whether substances used in your workplace that are not regulated by OSHA are hazardous, you may contact OSHA. (*See list of OSHA Offices at page 118.*)

Other OSHA regulations that might apply include the Air Contaminants standard, 29 CFR 1910.1000, the substance-specific standards, appropriate safety regulations such as the Hazardous Waste Operations and Emergency Response standard, 29 CFR 1910.120, paragraph (g)(2), and many construction and maritime standards.

What is a Permissible Exposure Limit (PEL)?

Employee exposure means exposure to a concentration of an airborne contaminant that would occur if the employee were not using respiratory protection. OSHA permissible exposure limits (PELs) establish the maximum level of a specific airborne hazard that an employee can be exposed to, averaged over an 8-hour workday (8-hour time-weighted average, or TWA) or over a specified portion of a workday (e.g., a 15-minute short-term exposure limit, or STEL). Likewise, the action level (AL), which is one-half the PEL, is calculated in the same manner as the PEL, and is the level at or above which provisions of substance-specific standards can be triggered. (PELs are listed in 29 CFR 1910.1000, and 1926.55. *See also the substance-specific standards for general industry, maritime, longshoring, and construction.*)

(d)(3)(i)(A) You must select respirators according to Assigned Protection Factors (APF)

Selection of respirators must be made in accordance with the assigned protection factor (APF) of the respirator, as well as the workplace and exposure factors. (*See final APF standard; 71 FR 50122.*)

APF means the workplace level of respiratory protection that a respirator or class of respirators is expected to provide to employees when the employer implements a continuing, effective respiratory protection program as specified by *29 CFR 1910.134*.

Employers must use the APFs listed in Table I, at page 24, to select a respirator that meets or exceeds the required level of employee protection. When using a combination respirator (e.g., airline respirators with an air-purifying filter), employers must ensure that the APF is appropriate to the mode of operation in which the respirator is being used.

A copy of the new APF table is provided below, at page 24, in section (d) of this guide. *Footnote 4 of Table I* relates to the testing of Powered Air-Purifying Respirators (PAPRs) and Supplied-air Respirators (SAR) with helmets or hoods to demonstrate that these respirators can perform at the higher APF of 1,000 instead of the overall APF of 25 for this class. As a result of OSHA's rulemaking, the 25/1000 APF is given to some hood/helmet PAPRs and supplied-air respirators (SARs).

(d)(3)(i)(B) You must select respirators after considering the Maximum Use Concentrations in your workplace under which respirators are used

Maximum use concentration (MUC) means the maximum atmospheric concentration of a hazardous substance from which an employee can be expected to be protected when wearing a respirator, and is determined by the assigned protection factor of the respirator or class of respirators and the exposure limit of the hazardous substance. The MUC usually can be determined mathematically by multiplying the assigned protection factor specified for a respirator by the permissible exposure limit, short-term exposure limit, ceiling limit, peak limit, or any other exposure limit used for the hazardous substance. Basically, under the MUC, employers must: (1) select a respirator for employee use that maintains the employee's exposure to the hazardous substance, when measured outside the respirator, at or below the MUC; (2) not apply MUCs to conditions that are immediately dangerous to life or health (IDLH); instead, they must use respirators listed for IDLH conditions in *paragraph (d)(2)* of the Respiratory Protection standard; and, (3) set the maximum MUC at that lower limit when the calculated MUC exceeds the IDLH level for a hazardous substance, or the performance limits of the cartridge or canister.

How to use APFs and MUCs

APFs are used to select the appropriate class of respirators that will provide the necessary level of protection under routine and reasonably foreseeable emergency situations. The airborne hazardous exposure can be from a particulate or a gas or vapor. The APF for the class of respirators will remain the same. The APF value can only be applied to a class of respirators when the respirators are properly selected and used in compliance with the Respiratory Protection standard (29 CFR 1910.134). Also, for gases and vapors, additional cartridges and canisters may by needed. (*see paragraph (d)(3)(iii);* see change schedules of this guide.)

OSHA PELs (permissible exposure limits) establish the maximum level of a specific airborne hazard that an employee can be exposed to, averaged over an 8-hour workday (8-hour time-weighted average, or TWA) or over a specified portion of a workday (for example, a 15-minute short-term exposure limit, or STEL). (PELs are listed in 29 CFR 1910.1000, and 1926.55. Also see the substance-specific standards for general industry and construction.)

The MUC for respirators is calculated by multiplying the APF for the respirator by the PEL. The MUC is the upper exposure limit at which the class of respirator is expected to provide protection. Whenever the exposures approach the MUC, then the employer should consider selecting the next higher class of respirators for the employees.

MUCs for mixtures must satisfy the following equation:

$E_m = (C_1 \text{ divided by } L_1 + C_2 \text{ divided by } L_2) + \ldots (C_n \text{ divided by } L_n)$

Where:

E_m is the equivalent exposure for the mixture
C is the concentration of a particulate contaminant
L is the exposure limit for that substance
The value of E_m shall not exceed unity (1).

There are exceptions to this equation, or situations in which it is inappropriate to use this equation. Examples of such situations are:

- Whenever an APF=10 times the PEL puts the employee into an IDLH atmosphere or puts them into a lower explosive limit (LEL) situation, then a negative pressure respirator must not be used.

- OSHA does not allow negative pressure respirators to be used for methylene chloride (except for emergency escape), so if employees are exposed above the PEL they are already in violation of the methylene chloride standard [(29 CFR 1910.1052(g)(2) rather than 1910.134(d)(3)(B)]. Using the MUC calculation for a half facepiece negative pressure respirator used for MeCl would be an example an inappropriate use of the MUC.

- For a mixture of toluene and xylene, a half facepiece respirator should be allowed to be used in a mixture situation as long as C1/L1 + C2/L2 was less than E times the APF (10), e.g., 300ppm Toluene /100ppm PEL + 650ppm Xylene/100ppm PEL = 9.5, so the respirator could be used "according to the MUC calculation." However, this concentration would be extremely irritating to the eyes, and a full facepiece would be more appropriate.

(d)(3)(ii) You must select respirators that are appropriate for the chemical state and physical form of the contaminant

You need different types of filters, cartridges, and canisters depending on whether dusts, fumes, mists, vapors, or gases are present in your workplace and depending on the kinds and concentrations of substances present. *(See paragraph (d)(1)(iii).)*

(d)(3)(iii) Respiratory protection for gases and vapors

For protection against gases and vapors, employers must provide:

A. an atmosphere-supplying respirator, or

B. an air-purifying respirator that:

1) has an NIOSH-certified end-of-service-life indicator (ESLI), or

2) if there is no ESLI, employers must calculate the service life of canisters and cartridges for employees who are wearing respirators.

You do not want to have situations where the canisters or cartridges become saturated and the gases or vapors break through, allowing the contaminants to get inside the respirator and into your workers' breathing zones.

What is an end-of-service-life indicator (ESLI)?

An ESLI is a mechanism for warning the user that a respirator is approaching the end of its ability to provide protection. The warning appears on the cartridge itself. For example, after a period of use, an indicator on a cartridge with sorbent material will signal that protection against organic vapors is approaching saturation or is no longer effective. (The ESLI for a carbon-monoxide canister involves a color change when the sorbent material is exhausted.)

The final standard requires the use of ESLIs where they are available and appropriate for the employer's workplace, whether or not warning properties exist for a contaminant. If there is no ESLI available, the employer is required to develop a cartridge/canister change schedule based on available information and data that describe the service life of the sorbent elements against the contaminant present in the employer's workplace and that will ensure that sorbent elements are replaced before they are exhausted. Reliance on odor thresholds and other warning properties is not permitted in the final rule as the sole basis for determining that an air-purifying respirator will afford adequate protection against exposure to gas and vapor contaminants.

To the extent that NIOSH-certified end of service-life indicators are available, OSHA finds that there are

considerable benefits to their use. Thus far, however, NIOSH has only certified ESLIs for a few cartridges or canisters (for example, mercury vapor, carbon monoxide, ethylene oxide and hydrogen sulfide). Therefore, employers are more likely to have to establish change schedules to ensure that cartridges and canisters are changed before their end-of-service-life.

Why not just rely on the worker's ability to detect the odor of the substance when the gas or vapor breaks through?

You may not rely on the detection of odor as protection against respiratory hazards posed by gases and vapors because:

- Most toxic substances do not have appropriate sensory (odor or irritant) warning properties.

- Some chemicals have odors that are only detectable above their established exposure limits, meaning that the employees will smell the chemical only after they have already been exposed to unsafe levels of the contaminant.

- An individual's ability to perceive particular odors may differ quite markedly from the population average due to any of a variety of innate, chronic, or acute physiological conditions. For example, about 10 percent of people have a markedly impaired sense of smell.

- There is no good screening mechanism to identify persons with sensory-receptor problems. Continuing exposure to the odor usually results in diminution or even disappearance of the smell sensation. This phenomenon is known as olfactory fatigue. When this happens, the employee unknowingly gets used to the contaminant breaking through the cartridge/canister and loses the ability to detect its smell.

What must be considered when developing change schedules?

Employers must develop cartridge-change schedules based on available data or information that can be relied upon to ensure that cartridges are changed before the end of their useful service life.

You need to consider the following factors in developing change schedules:

- ❏ The contaminants the respirator is to protect against.

- ❏ The concentrations of contaminants in the work area.

- ❏ Frequency of use (e.g., is the respirator used continuously or intermittently throughout the shift);

- ❏ Temperature, humidity and air flow through the cartridge or canister.

- ❏ Employees' work rates.

- ❏ The presence of other potentially interfering substances.

You should assume worst-case conditions to avoid breakthrough earlier than anticipated.

You should document the information relied upon and the basis for the change schedules you use in your written respiratory protection program.

Where can I get help for developing change schedules?

You need to consult with your respirator supplier or manufacturer for guidance on developing change schedules specific to your work conditions. Some suppliers have prepared materials that may assist you with developing change schedules for your worksite. Other possible sources of help include your trade associations, which may be gathering published information, such as breakthrough test data (i.e., how long it takes a substance to break through the cartridge or canister and get into the facepiece). There is a model (the MultiVapor model) for estimating cartridge and canister breakthrough periods for gases and/or vapors. The software is available from NIOSH. (*See information from NIOSH on the MultiVapor model at Attachment 5 in this guide.*)

Furthermore, a specific rule of thumb also will help employers determine cartridge and canister schedules. These are as follows:

Rule of Thumb

Experimental work can allow for a generalization or "rule of thumb" that broadly covers service life of cartridges exposed to chemicals. One such Rule of Thumb for estimating vapor cartridge service life is found in chapter 36 of the American Industrial Hygiene Association publication "The Occupational Environment – Its Evaluation and Control."

It suggests that:

- If the chemical's boiling point is > 70° C and the concentration is less than 200 ppm you can expect a service life of 8 hours at a normal work rate.

- Service life is inversely proportional to work rate.

- Reducing concentration by a factor of 10 will increase service life by a factor of 5.

- Humidity above 85% will reduce service life by 50%.

These generalizations can be used in concert with other methods of predicting service life for specific contaminants.

Whenever a cartridge has become saturated or a contaminant has broken through the cartridge, the respirator must be taken out of service so that the cartridge can be replaced.

In general, The MultiVapor model (Attachment 5) and The Rule of Thumb can be used to calculate the service life of a respirator cartridge or canister, when the calculations are made using information about the canisters or cartridges themselves in combination with additional information about the workplace conditions. The information about the canisters or cartridges may be obtained from the respirator manufacturers. Calculations for either the MultiVapor model or the Rule of Thumb require information about the workplace, as well. The Rule of Thumb provides a rough estimate of the service life. Attachment 5 is a NIOSH table of cartridges and canisters by APFs that may provide assistance as well.

(d)(3)(iv) Respiratory protection for particulates

What are my options for protection against particulates?

You have three options:

- Atmosphere-supplying respirators.

- Air-purifying respirators (including filtering face-pieces)

  - with filters certified by NIOSH under 30 CFR part 11 as high efficiency particulate air filters (HEPA), or

  - filters certified by NIOSH under 42 CFR part 84.

- Air-purifying respirators with any filter certified for particulates by NIOSH for protection against contaminants consisting primarily of particles with mass median aerodynamic diameters (MMAD) of at least two micrometers (µm).

Local OSHA offices can help to determine whether or not contaminants in your workplace consist primarily of particles of two micrometers or more.

What types of particulate filters are available for air-purifying respirators (APRs)?

Particulate-removing filters are used to protect employees from toxic dusts and fibers, such as lead and asbestos, fumes, mists, and radioactive and biological materials (such as grain dusts, bacteria, and viruses). Powered and non-powered APRs require different particulate filters. Appropriate protection against particulates for powered APRs is provided by HEPA filters.

There are nine filter types for use with non-powered APRs approved by NIOSH, and they are based on three levels of filter efficiency and three levels of resistance to degradation by oil. The three levels of filter efficiency are 95, 99, and 99.97 percent and are referred to as 95, 99 and 100 filters, respectively. The efficiency of a filter is based upon the percent of the most penetrating size particle (0.3 micrometers in diameter) that it can exclude (e.g., a 95 filter can exclude 95% of particles of this size).

The three levels of oil resistance are N (not oil resistant), R (oil resistant) and P (oilproof). The most common commercially available cartridges are the "N95" (not oil resistant and 95 percent efficient) and "P100" (oilproof and 99.97 percent efficient). N-series

Particulate Respirator Filter Type	Percentage (%) of 0.3 µm airborne particles filtered out	Not resistant to oil	Somewhat resistant to oil	Strongly resistant to oil (oilproof)
N95	95	X		
N99	99	X		
N100	99.97	X		
R95	95		X	
R99	99		X	
R100	99.97		X	
P95	95			X
P99	99			X
P100	99.97			X

The P100 is comparable to the HEPA filter that is used with PAPRs.

OSHA®
Occupational Safety and
Health Administration

filters are not required to demonstrate resistance to the potentially "degrading" effects of oils and are, therefore, not intended for use in workplace atmospheres that contain oily aerosols. In this context, "degrading" means that exposure to an agent may cause an increase in filter penetration measured under laboratory test conditions. R and P series filters must demonstrate oil resistance when tested with dioctyl phthalate (DOP), which is described as a "highly degrading" oil aerosol. As a result, both R and P filters can be used in workplace atmospheres that contain oily aerosols, as well as those that do not.

The nine different types of particulate respirator filter types are listed in the table on page 22.

Do I need to use particulate filters with ESLI?

There are no ESLI for particulate-removing filters. Workers should be trained to change the filters when they experience difficulty breathing through the filter. This is usually an indication that the filter has become loaded with particulate.

Where can I go for help?

Sources of help include:

- *NIOSH Respirator Selection Logic.* U.S. Department of Health and Human Services, Public Health Service, Centers for Disease Control, National Institute for Occupational Safety and Health. Request DHHS (NIOSH) Publication No. 2005-100. NIOSH also has a help line. The telephone number is 1-800-35 NIOSH or http://www.cdc.gov/niosh/docs/2005-100/default.html
- American National Standard for Respiratory Protection (ANSI Z88.2). American National Standards Institute, 11 West 42nd Street, New York, New York, 10036. See: global.ihs.ANSI Z88.2
- Respirator manufacturers provide advice through product literature, sales staff, and telephone help lines. The Industrial Safety Equipment Association (ISEA) has contact information. ISEA can be reached at: 1901 N. Moore Street, Suite 808, Arlington, Virginia, 22209, or (703) 525-1695.
- Chemical manufacturers may provide information on the nature and properties of substances to which your employees may be exposed. You should be able to obtain information from the Material Safety Data Sheets (MSDSs) provided by the supplier of the substance.
- You can contact the American Conference of Governmental Industrial Hygienists (ACGIH), 6500 Glenway Ave., Bldg. D-7, Cincinnati, Ohio, 45211-4438, for advice and information on exposure measurement and estimation and other related industrial hygiene subjects. ACGIH has published the ACGIH Ventilation Manual, which contains calculations applied to certain situations to estimate employee exposures.

- You can also contact the American Industrial Hygiene Association (AIHA), 2700 Prosperity Ave., Suite 250, Fairfax, Virginia, 22031, for advice and information on exposure measurement and estimation. Members of AIHA's Exposure Assessment Strategies Committee are knowledgeable in worker exposure measurement and estimation. (*See: http://www.aiha.org/Content.*)
- The National Library of Medicine provides free online help about chemical hazards. Through TOXNET, located at: http://toxnet.nlm.nih.gov, you can search a number of databases on toxicology, hazardous chemicals, hazardous biological atmospheres, and other related subjects for information on respiratory hazards.

CHECKLIST FOR RESPIRATOR SELECTION

√ Check that the following has been done at your facility:

❑ Respiratory hazards in your workplace have been identified and evaluated.

❑ Employee exposures that have not been, or cannot be, evaluated must be considered IDLH.

❑ Respirators are NIOSH-certified, and used under the conditions of certification.

❑ Respirators are selected based on the workplace hazards evaluated and workplace and user factors affecting respirator performance and reliability.

❑ Respirators are selected based on the APFs and calculated MUCs.

❑ A sufficient number of respirator sizes and models are provided for selection purposes.

For IDLH atmospheres:

❑ Full facepiece pressure demand SARs with auxiliary SCBA unit or full facepiece pressure demand SCBAs, with a minimum service life of 30 minutes, are provided.

❑ Respirators used for escape only are NIOSH-certified for the atmosphere in which they will be used.

❑ Oxygen deficient atmospheres must be *considered IDLH (d)(2)(B)(iii).*

For Non-IDLH atmospheres:

❑ Respirators selected are appropriate for the APFs and MUCs.

❑ Respirators selected are appropriate for the chemical nature and physical form of the contaminant.

❑ Air-purifying respirators used for protection against gases and vapors are equipped with ESLIs or a change schedule has been implemented.

❑ Air-purifying respirators used for protection against particulates are equipped with NIOSH-certified HEPA filters or other filters certified by NIOSH for particulates under 42 CFR part 84.

Table I: Assigned Protection Factors [5]

Type of Respirator [1,2]	Quarter Mask	Half Mask	Full Facepiece	Helmet/Hood	Loose-Fitting Facepiece
1. Air-Purifying Respirator	5	10[3]	50	—	—
2. Powered Air-Purifying Respirator (PAPR)	—	50	1,000	25/1,000 [4]	25
3. Supplied-Air Respirator (SAR) or Airline Respirator					
• Demand mode	—	10	50	—	—
• Continuous flow mode	—	50	1,000	25/1,000 [4]	25
• Pressure-demand or other positive pressure mode	—	50	1,000	—	—
4. Self-Contained Breathing Apparatus (SCBA)					
• Demand mode	—	10	50	50	—
• Pressure-demand or other positive pressure mode (e.g., open/closed circuit)	—	—	10,000	10,000	—

Notes:

[1] Employers may select respirators assigned for use in higher workplace concentrations of a hazardous substance for use at lower concentrations of that substance, or when required respirator use is independent of concentration.

[2] The assigned protection factors in Table I are only effective when the employer implements a continuing, effective respirator program as required by this section (29 CFR 1910.134), including training, fit testing, maintenance, and use requirements.

[3] This APF category includes filtering facepieces, and half masks with elastomeric facepieces.

[4] The employer must have evidence provided by the respirator manufacturer that testing of these respirators demonstrates performance at a level of protection of 1,000 or greater to receive an APF of 1,000. This level of performance can best be demonstrated by performing a WPF or SWPF study or equivalent testing. Absent such testing, all other PAPRs and SARs with helmets/hoods are to be treated as loose-fitting facepiece respirators, and receive an APF of 25.

[5] These APFs do not apply to respirators used solely for escape. For escape respirators used in association with specific substances covered by 29 CFR 1910 subpart Z, employers must refer to the appropriate substance-specific standards in that subpart. Escape respirators for other IDLH atmospheres are specified by 29 CFR 1910.134(d)(2)(ii).

Occupational Safety and
Health Administration

Air-purifying respirators

Air-purifying respirators, which remove contaminants from the air.

Half mask Filtering Facepiece Dust mask
APF=10
Needs to be fit tested

Half mask Elastomeric Respirator
APF=10
Needs to be fit tested

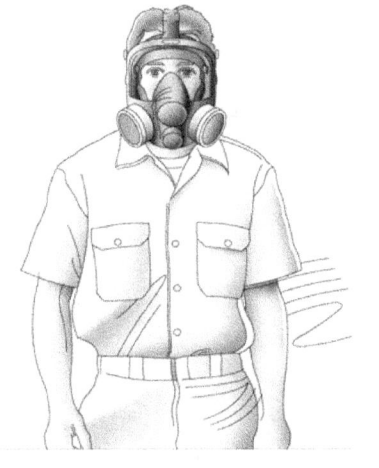

Full Facepiece Elastomeric Respirator
APF=50
Needs to be fit tested

Original Illustrations created by Attiliis & Associates

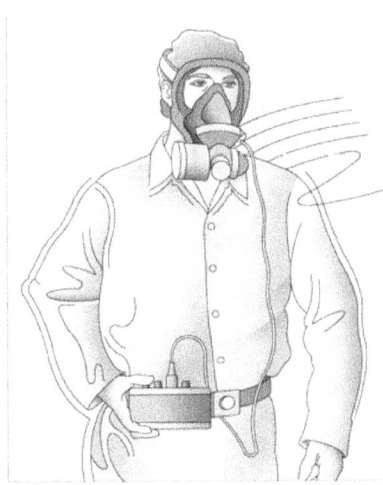

Tight-Fitting Full Facepiece Powered Air-Purifying Respirator (PAPR)
APF=1,000
Needs to be fit tested

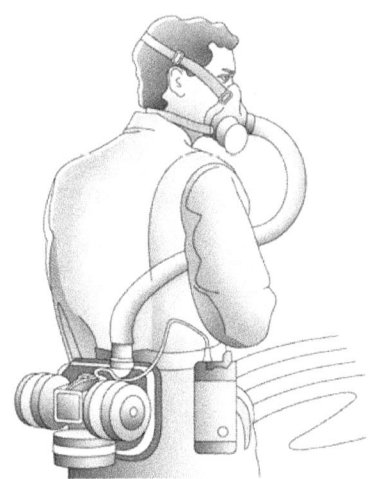

Tight-Fitting Half Facepiece Powered Air-Purifying Respirator (PAPR)
APF=50
Needs to be fit tested

Examples of Air-purifying respirators that can not be fit tested because they are loose-fitting

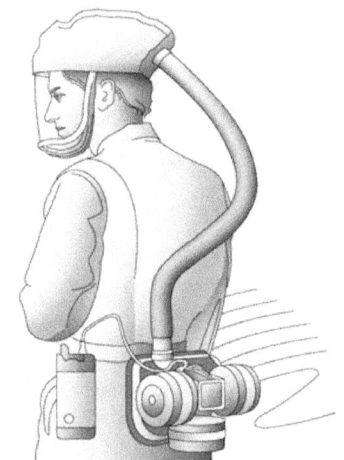

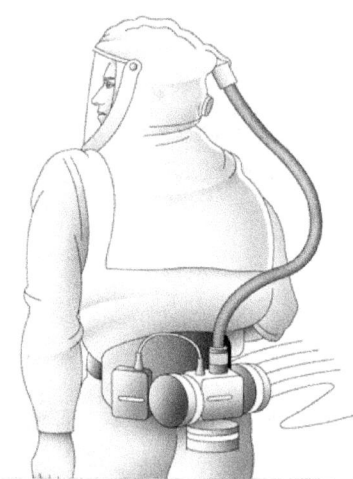

Loose-Fitting Powered Air-Purifying Respirator (PAPR)
APF=25

Hooded Powered Air-Purifying Respirator (PAPR)
APF=25 (1,000)*

Atmosphere-supplying respirators

Atmosphere-supplying respirators, which provide clean air from an uncontaminated source

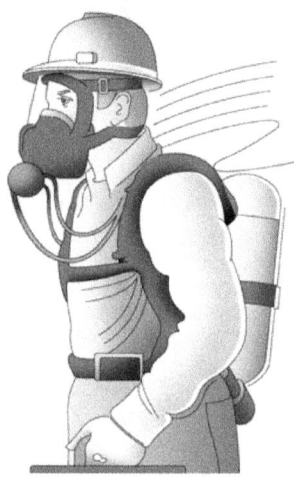

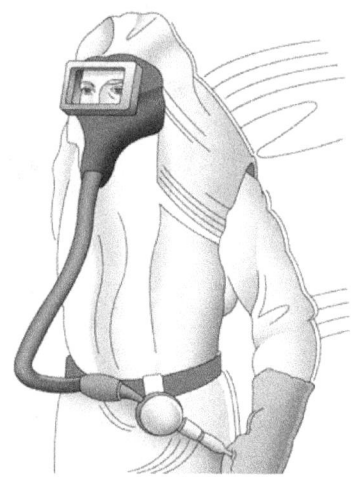

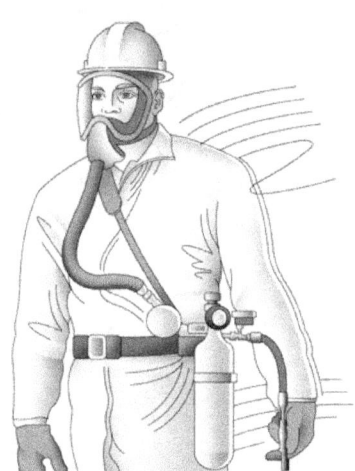

Tight-fitting Self-Contained Breathing Apparatus (SCBA) pressure-demand mode
APF=10,000
Demand mode
APF=50
Needs to be fit tested

Tight-fitting Abrasive Blasting Respirator Continuous flow
APF=25/1,000*
SAR Full Facepiece
*Needs to be fit tested***

Tight-fitting Atmosphere-Supplying Respirator with an auxiliary escape bottle
APF=10,000 in escape mode only; otherwise APF=1,000
Full facepiece
Needs to be fit tested

* APF=25/1,000; Footnote 4 in the APF Table.
** One type of SAR Hood (not depicted) is a SAR with a loose hood; a loose-fitting SAR Hood looks much like this example, but without the tight-fitting facepiece, and does not need to be fit tested. For a loose-fitting facepiece SAR Hood the APF=25 unless the respirator qualifies for a higher APF under Footnote 4.

OSHA®
Occupational Safety and Health Administration

Table II: Oxygen Deficient Atmospheres

Altitude (ft)	Oxygen deficient atmospheres (% O₂) for which the employer may rely on any atmosphere-supplying respirator
Less than 3001	16.0-19.5
3001-4000	16.4-19.5
4001-5000	17.1-19.5
5001-6000	17.8-19.5
6001-7000	18.5-19.5
7001-8000[1]	19.3-19.5

[1] Above 8,000 feet the exception does not apply. Oxygen-enriched breathing air must be supplied above 14,000 feet.

Section (e): Medical evaluation

This section of the Respiratory Protection standard requires employers to implement medical evaluations to determine an employee's ability to use a respirator. This requirement is necessary because using a respirator may place a burden on an employee's health. This burden varies according to a number of factors, such as the weight and breathing resistance of the respirator and the workplace conditions under which the respirator is worn.

Examples of some medical conditions that may be associated with sudden incapacitation, or may interfere with safe use of a respirator or specific type of respirator, include:

- Cardiovascular and respiratory disease, such as high blood pressure, angina, asthma, chronic bronchitis, or emphysema.
- Cardiovascular damage caused by heart attack or stroke.
- Reduced lung function caused by factors such as smoking or prior exposure to respiratory hazards.
- Neurological disorders, such as epilepsy.
- Musculoskeletal disorders, such as lower back pain.
- Psychological conditions, such as claustrophobia and severe anxiety.

This list provides examples of only **some** medical conditions that **may** interfere with safe use of a respirator, or specific type of respirator. In addition, certain medications may interfere with safe use of a respirator.

(e)(1) Employer provided medical evaluations

The employer must provide an employee with a medical evaluation to determine his or her ability to use a respirator. If an employee refuses to be medically evaluated for the use of a respirator, he or she cannot be assigned to a job that requires a respirator.

When do I need to provide an employee with a medical evaluation?

The medical evaluation must be provided **before** the employee is fit tested and uses the respirator in your workplace for the first time.

Are medical evaluations required for all types of respirators?

Medical evaluations are required for both positive pressure and negative pressure respirators. When elastomeric or supplied-air respirators are worn voluntarily by employees (not required by you or OSHA), you must ensure that the employees are medically able to wear the respirators and that they are provided with the necessary information as required in the *standard*. (*See Attachment 2 at page 61.*) The procedures for making this medical determination must be part of your written respiratory protection program. When your employees voluntarily wear dust masks (filtering facepiece respirators), no medical examination is required.

Do I need to provide medical evaluations for seasonal and temporary employees?

If seasonal or temporary employees are required to wear a respirator, you must provide them with medical evaluations. The frequency or length of an employee's term of employment does not affect the requirement for medical evaluations.

(e)(2) Medical evaluation procedures

This portion of the standard specifies that the medical evaluation can be performed by using the mandatory portions of the medical questionnaire found in *Appendix C* of the Respiratory Protection standard. The mandatory portions of this Appendix in the final standard are under:

Appendix C to § 1910.134: OSHA Respirator Medical Evaluation Questionnaire (Mandatory)

Appendix C - Part A. Section 1. (Mandatory) - every employee who has been selected to use any type of respirator must answer all 12 questions.

Appendix C - Part A. Section 2. (Mandatory) - Questions 1 through 9 must be answered by every employee who has been selected to use any type of respirator. Questions 10 to 15 must also be answered by every employee who has been selected to use either a full-facepiece respirator or a self-contained breathing apparatus (SCBA). For employees who have been selected to use other types of respirators, answering questions 10 - 15 is optional.

All medical evaluations can be performed using the medical questionnaire of the standard, in *Appendix C*, or by a medical examination that obtains the same information as the medical questionnaire.

Question number 1 in *Part A. Section 1*, and question number 9 in *Part A. Section 2* collect personal historic data.

If an employee gives a positive answer to question number 9 in *Part A. Section 2*, the employer must allow the employee to contact the physician or other licensed healthcare professional (PLHCP).

There is a non-mandatory section of the medical questionnaire, *Part B of Appendix C* of the standard.

Identification of a Medical Professional

Employers must identify a physician or another licensed health care professional (PLHCP) to perform the medical evaluations.

Who can perform a medical evaluation?

Physicians are not the only health care professionals allowed to perform medical evaluations for respirator use. The Respiratory Protection standard allows any PLHCP to administer the medical questionnaire (described below) or to conduct the medical examination if doing so is within the scope of the PLHCP's license. You must check with PLHCPs in your local area to see if performing the medical evaluation is within the scope of their professional license. Or you may check with your state licensing board.

Can a nurse perform a medical evaluation?

Any health care professional, including a nurse, who qualifies as a PLHCP can perform a medical evaluation. If a nurse does not qualify as a PLHCP, he or she may still be able to perform a medical evaluation if he or she is doing so under the supervision of a physician, and the physician performs the final review of the assessment.

Can an employee request to see his or her own physician for a medical evaluation?

Yes, however, you are not required by the standard to comply with this request. If employees select their own physicians, you will need to maintain contact with each physician, and you will need to send each physician the supplemental information described in paragraph (e)(5) of the standard. You must allow the employee to be evaluated during the employee's normal working hours or at a time that is convenient to the employee, and you also are responsible for paying for this service (even if the employee has coverage under an insurance plan).

The Medical Questionnaire: The medical questionnaire is designed to identify general medical conditions that could place employees who use respirators at risk of serious medical consequences. If you choose to use the medical questionnaire to conduct the medical evaluation, you must use the questionnaire contained in *Appendix C to § 1910.134: OSHA Respirator Medical Evaluation Questionnaire (Mandatory)* of the Respiratory Protection standard. A copy of the standard is in Attachment 3 of this guide.

You may choose to use medical examinations in place of the questionnaire, but you are not required to do so. Although the questionnaire does not have to be administered during the medical examination, the PLHCP must obtain the same information from the employee that is contained in the questionnaire.

(e)(3) Follow-up medical examinations

Employers must provide follow-up examinations for employees who give positive answers to any of the questions numbered *1 through 8 in Part A. Section 2, Appendix C to § 1910.134*. Employees who will be using SCBAs or full-face respirators will be asked questions 10 through 15 in this same section. Also, employers must provide a follow-up examination if the medical examination indicates that one is necessary for any other reason specified by the examining PLHCP.

As part of any medical examination, the PLHCP may include any tests, consultations, or diagnostic procedures that, in the opinion of the examining PLHCP, are necessary to make a final determination about an employee's ability to use a respirator. In some cases, all that might be needed is a phone call to the employee from the PLHCP to clarify an issue from the questionnaire.

If the PLHCP is not a physician, some medical issues may arise during follow-up examinations that may be outside the scope of the PLHCP's license. In such cases, a qualified physician or other licensed healthcare provider with appropriate licensure must be involved.

(e)(4) Administration of questionnaires and examinations

What procedures exist for administering the medical evaluation?

When you provide a medical evaluation program:

- You must protect the confidentiality of the employee who is being evaluated.

- The medical evaluation must be given during an employee's normal work hours or at a time and place convenient to the employee.

- The employee must understand the questions on the medical questionnaire.

Who pays for the medical evaluation?

You must pay for the medical evaluation and any related expenses, including travel costs, incurred by your employee during the evaluation.

How can I ensure that a employee's medical evaluation remains confidential?

You must provide your employees with instructions on how to deliver or send the completed questionnaire to the PLHCP who will review it. This can be done, for example, by supplying them with stamped, pre-addressed envelopes for mailing their completed questionnaires to the PLHCP.

If an employee does not speak English or cannot read, how can I make sure that he or she understands the questions on the medical questionnaire?

You can send the employee directly to a PLHCP who is able to help the employee fill out the questionnaire. For non-English speakers, you may want to consider supplying an interpreter to help the PLHCP interpret the questionnaire for your employee. The standard does not require you to hire a professional interpreter; instead, you may use an English-speaking family member or friend of the employee, or another employee who speaks both English and the employee's language, who can help the employee fill out the questionnaire.

Employee's Right to Contact the PLHCP

The standard requires you to inform employees that a PLHCP is available to discuss the medical questionnaire with them, and to allow employees to discuss the results of their questionnaire with the PLHCP. This discussion will enable employees and PLHCPs to clarify questions that were asked on the questionnaire, and for employees to explain answers that they provided.

How can I notify employees about how to contact the PLHCP?

You could post the PLHCP's name and telephone number in a location that is easily accessible to all employees (such as a lunchroom or break area). You could also include the information in a separate sheet with the medical questionnaire.

(e)(5) Supplemental information for the PLHCP

This portion of the Respiratory Protection standard requires you to provide the PLHCP with specific information to be used to make the determination about an employee's ability to use a respirator.

This information includes:

- The type and weight of the respirator to be worn by the worker.
- The duration and frequency of respirator use (including use for rescue and escape).
- The level of physical effort that the employee would be expending while wearing a respirator.
- Additional personal protective clothing and equipment that the employee would wear.
- The temperature and humidity extremes that may be encountered in the work environment where respirator use is required.
- In addition, you must provide the PLHCP with the following:
  - A copy of your written respiratory protection program.
  - A copy of the Respiratory Protection standard.

Why do I need to provide the PLHCP with a copy of the written respiratory protection program and the Respiratory Protection standard?

This requirement helps ensure that PLHCPs have a thorough understanding of their duties and responsibilities in the medical evaluation process. Your written respiratory protection program will provide the PLHCP with critical information about the working conditions that could increase the burden placed on the employee's health during respirator use.

Does the PLHCP need to visit the worksite to perform a medical evaluation?

No, the supplemental information required in this portion of the standard should be sufficient for the PLHCP to make a valid recommendation on the employee's ability to wear a respirator. OSHA, however, encourages PLHCPs to visit the worksite if they believe the information obtained there would be useful to them.

If I select a new PLHCP, do I need to have my employees reevaluated?

No, but you must make sure that the new PLHCP has the information required in this section. You must either provide the information directly to the new PLHCP, or you must make sure that the information is transferred from the former PLHCP to the new PLHCP.

How often do I need to provide the PLHCP with supplemental information?

You need to supply the information to the PLHCP only when the conditions of respirator use change.

(e)(6) Medical determination

This portion of the standard requires you to obtain a recommendation from the PLHCP about the employee's ability to use a respirator. The PLHCP's recommendation must be in writing, and it must provide only the following information:

- A determination of whether or not the employee is medically able to use a respirator.

- Any limitations on respirator use related to the medical condition of the employee or to the workplace conditions in which the respirator will be used.

- The need, if any, for follow-up medical evaluations.

- A statement that the PLHCP has provided the employee with a copy of the PLHCP's written recommendation.

Note that you are required to have the PLHCP provide a copy of the written recommendation to each employee.

Who is responsible for making the final decision about an employee's ability to wear a respirator?

You are responsible for making the final determination. The PLHCP's opinion is an important factor that you must consider in making this determination.

Is the information from the medical evaluation confidential, or can the PLHCP share this information with me?

The PLHCP must keep strictly confidential any information revealed during the medical evaluation; your access is limited to the information contained in the PLHCP's written recommendation.

Can I receive a copy of the employee's completed medical questionnaire?

No, the completed questionnaire is a medical record and must be kept confidential.

Negative Pressure Respirators and Powered Air-Purifying Respirators (PAPR): If the PLHCP determines that an employee is unable to wear a negative pressure respirator, perhaps because of a breathing problem such as asthma or bronchitis, but would be able to wear a powered air-purifying respirator (PAPR), you must provide the employee with a PAPR. If, however, the PLHCP determines in a subsequent medical evaluation that the employee can wear a negative pressure respirator, you no longer need to provide the employee with a PAPR. *(See 29 CFR 1910.1034(e)(6)(ii).)*

(e)(7) Additional medical evaluations

This portion of the standard requires you to provide an employee with additional medical evaluations whenever the following events occur:

- The employee reports symptoms related to his or her ability to use a respirator.

- The PLHCP, respiratory protection program administrator, or supervisor, determines that a medical reevaluation is necessary.

- Information from the respiratory protection program suggests a need for reevaluation.

- Workplace conditions (such as protective clothing, temperature, or level of work effort) have changed so that an increased physiological burden is placed on the employee.

- The results of the medical examination reveal that additional medical evaluations are necessary.

The results of the medical examination reveal that additional medical evaluations are necessary. Do I need to provide my employees with a medical reevaluation annually or according to some other fixed schedule?

No, however, you must provide medical reevaluations in accordance with the PLHCP's recommendation.

Do I need to provide an employee who is unable to use a respirator with an alternative job at no loss of pay and other benefits?

The Respiratory Protection standard does not require that workers receive such benefits; however, other OSHA substance-specific standards may contain such a requirement.

Occupational Safety and Health Administration

CHECKLIST FOR MEDICAL EVALUATION

√ Check that the following has been done at your facility:

❏ All employees have been evaluated to determine their ability to wear a respirator prior to being fit tested for or wearing a respirator for the first time in your workplace.

❏ A physician or other licensed healthcare professional (PLHCP) has been identified to perform the medical evaluations.

❏ The medical evaluations obtain the information requested in *Sections 1 and 2, Part A of Appendix C of the standard, 29 CFR 1910.134. (See Attachment 3 at page 67)*

❏ Employees are provided follow-up medical exams if they answer positively to any of *questions 1 through 8 in Section 2, Part A of Appendix C* of the standard, or if their medical examination reveals that a follow-up exam is needed.

❏ Medical evaluations are administered confidentially during normal work hours, and in a manner that is understandable to employees.

❏ Employees are provided the opportunity to discuss the medical evaluation results with the PLHCP.

❏ The following supplemental information is provided to the PLHCP before he or she makes a decision about respirator use:
  • Type and weight of the respirator.
  • Duration and frequency of respirator use.
  • Expected physical work effort.
  • Additional protective clothing to be worn.
  • Potential temperature and humidity extremes.
  • Written copies of the respiratory protection program and the Respiratory Protection standard are provided to the PLHCP.

❏ Written recommendations are obtained from the PLHCP regarding each employee's ability to wear a respirator, and that the PLHCP has given the worker a copy of these recommendations.

❏ Employees who are medically unable to wear a negative pressure respirator are provided with a powered air-purifying respirator (PAPR) if they are found by the PLHCP to be medically able to use a PAPR. *(29 CFR 1910.1034(e)(6)(ii).)*

Employees are given additional medical evaluations when:

❏ The employee reports symptoms related to his or her ability to use a respirator.

❏ The PLHCP, respiratory protection program administrator, or supervisor determines that a medical reevaluation is necessary.

❏ Information from the respiratory protection program suggests a need for reevaluation.

❏ Workplace conditions have changed in a way that could potentially place an increased physiological burden on the employee.

Section (f): Fit testing

This section of the Respiratory Protection standard requires you to conduct fit testing on all employees who are required to wear a respirator that includes a tight-fitting facepiece. Fit testing is a procedure used to determine how well a respirator "fits"—that is, whether the respirator forms a seal on the user's face. If a good facepiece-to-face seal is not achieved, the respirator will provide a lower level of protection than it was designed to provide. For example, without a good seal, the respirator can allow contaminants to leak into the user's breathing air. The APFs for the specific classes of respirators in the final Respiratory Protection standard (*Table I: Assigned Protection Factors*) only apply if the respirators are properly selected and used in compliance with the full respirator program, including initial fit testing when necessary. Fit testing must be performed before initial use and at least annually thereafter.

This section also describes:

• What types of respirators must be fit tested.

• How often fit testing must be conducted.

• What procedures must be used.

• How the results of fit testing should be used to guide respirator selection.

Examples of respirators that need to be fit tested (tight-fitting facepieces)

Air-purifying respirators remove contaminants from the air

Half mask Filtering Facepiece Dust mask
APF=10
Needs to be fit tested

Half mask Elastomeric Respirator
APF=10
Needs to be fit tested

Examples of respirators that need to be fit tested (tight-fitting facepieces) *(continued)*

Full Facepiece Elastomeric Respirator
APF=50
Needs to be fit tested

Tight-Fitting Full Facepiece Powered Air-Purifying Respirator (PAPR)
APF=1,000
Needs to be fit tested

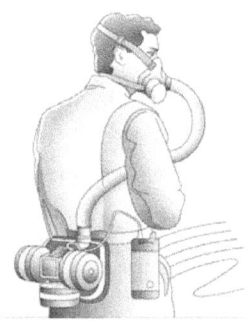

Tight-Fitting Half Facepiece Powered Air-Purifying Respirator (PAPR)
APF=50
Needs to be fit tested

Atmosphere-supplied respirator Full Facepiece Elastomeric with an auxiliary escape bottle
APF=10,000 in escape mode only; otherwise APF=1,000
Needs to be fit tested

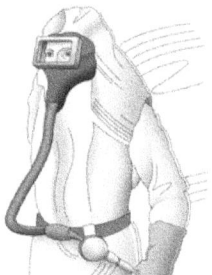

Abrasive Blasting Respirator; Atmosphere-supplying respirator Full Facepiece Elastomeric
APF=25/1,000*
Needs to be fit tested;
Continuous flow

* Footnote 4 of the APF Table

Examples of air-purifying respirators that can not be fit tested because they are loose-fitting

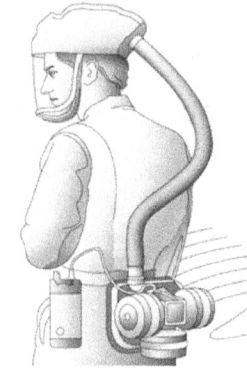

Loose-Fitting Powered Air-Purifying Respirator (PAPR)
APF=25

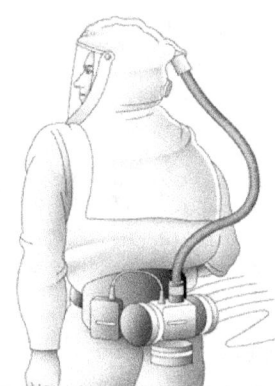

Hooded Powered Air-Purifying Respirator (PAPR)
APF=25 1,000*

* Footnote 4 of the APF Table

What is a tight-fitting facepiece?

A tight-fitting facepiece is intended to form a complete seal with the respirator wearer's face. This seal must be sufficiently tight to prevent any contaminants in the work environment from leaking around the edges of the facepiece into the user's breathing air.

In contrast, a loose-fitting facepiece is specifically designed to form a partial seal with the user's face. Such a facepiece typically covers at least the head and includes a system through which clean air is distributed into the breathing zone. For example, hoods and helmets are loose-fitting facepieces. Such equipment does not rely on a tight facepiece-to-face seal to protect the employee, and is useful for employees with facial hair or other physical characteristics that make it difficult to wear a tight-fitting facepiece.

**Occupational Safety and
Health Administration**

Examples of tight-fitting facepieces

Half mask Filtering Facepiece
Dust mask
APF=10

Half mask Elastomeric
Respirator
APF=10

Full Facepiece Elastomeric
Respirator
APF=50

What are positive pressure and negative pressure respirators?

Positive pressure respirators maintain positive air pressure inside the facepiece throughout the user's breathing cycle. That is, the air pressure inside the facepiece remains greater than the air pressure outside the facepiece. Thus, any leakage around the facepiece seal should result in air escaping from inside the facepiece to the outside environment rather than worksite contaminants leaking into the facepiece and breathing air.

In contrast, a negative pressure respirator will have a lower air pressure inside the facepiece than outside during inhalation. If the facepiece-to-face seal leaks on these types of respirators, air contaminants will be drawn into the breathing air.

Examples of the two major types of respirators that require fit testing, negative pressure (air-purifying) and positive pressure (atmosphere-supplying)

Air-purifying respirator, which removes contaminants from the air Half mask Filtering Facepiece; Dust mask
Needs to be fit tested
APF=10

Self-Contained Breathing Apparatus (SCBA)
Atmosphere-supplying, or Supplied-air respirator (SAR), which provides clean air from an uncontaminated source
Needs to be fit tested
APF=10,000

What is quantitative fit testing (QNFT)?

Quantitative fit testing is a method of measuring the amount of leakage into a respirator. It is a numeric assessment of how well a respirator fits a particular individual. To quantitatively fit test a respirator, sampling probes or other measuring devices must be placed to measure aerosol concentrations both outside and on the inside of the respirator facepiece.

The respirator wearer then performs the user seal checks followed by the selected QNFT. Basically, a user seal check is a quick and easy way for employees to verify that they have put on their respirators correctly and that the respirators are working properly. More detailed information on the user seal check is provided in Section (g): Use of Respirators, at page 41.

- For the generated aerosol QNFT, the respirator wearer stands inside a "test chamber" (booth or hood), where a nontoxic aerosol is introduced into the air. Measurements are then taken of the aerosol concentration both inside the test chamber and inside the respirator. An assessment of the quantitative fit is made based on the ratio of the aerosol concentration inside the test chamber to the concentration inside the facepiece.

- For the condensation nuclei counter QNFT, ambient air particles are used as the test aerosol with measurements made of their concentration outside and inside the facepiece, and an assessment is made of the quantitative fit of the facepiece.

- The controlled negative pressure QNFT method uses an instrument to exhaust air from inside the respirator facepiece to maintain a constant negative pressure. The measurement of the exhaust stream required to maintain a constant negative pressure yields a measure of leakage into the facepiece.

- Detailed protocols for quantitative fit testing are provided under Appendix A of the standard. *(See Attachment 3 at page 67.)*

What is qualitative fit testing (QLFT)?

Qualitative fit testing is a non-numeric pass/fail test that relies on the respirator wearer's response to a substance ("test agent") used in the test to determine respirator fit.

In qualitative fit testing, after performing user seal checks, the respirator wearer stands in an enclosure and a test agent is introduced. Such test agents are:

- Banana oil (Isoamyl acetate)

- Saccharin

- Bitrex

- Irritant smoke (no enclosure)

In qualitative fit testing, using irritant smoke as the test agent, there is no enclosure.

If the individual can detect the test agent, this indicates that the agent leaked into the facepiece and that the respirator has failed the test because a good facepiece-to-face seal has not been achieved. If the employee cannot successfully complete the qualitative test with a particular respirator, the employee must then be tested with another make, size, or model of respirator.

Detailed protocols for qualitative fit testing are in *Appendix A* of the standard. *(See Attachment 3 at page 67.)*

What is the fit factor?

The fit factor is a quantitative measure of how well a particular respirator fits (or provides protection to) an individual. It is the ratio of the concentration of a contaminant in the environment to the concentration inside the mask.

Fit factors are obtained from quantitative fit testing. For example, if an employee was in a test chamber that contained 300 ppm of aerosol and 3 ppm of the test agent was found inside the mask, the fit factor would be equal to 100.

Qualitative Fit Testing and User Seal Checking

Qualitative Fit Test

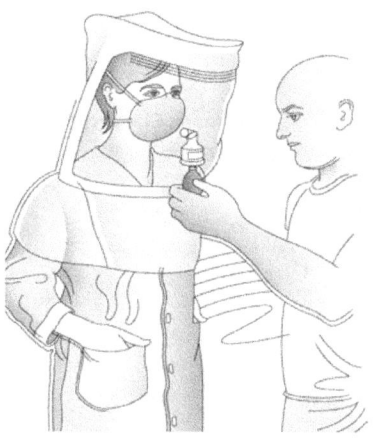

User seal check (paragraph (g))

A user seal check is not a fit test. The user seal check is one step an employee must take before any fit testing is performed and before the employee uses the respirator in the workplace.

Occupational Safety and Health Administration

(f)(1) Respirators that require fit testing

You must ensure that quantitative or qualitative fit testing is conducted for all employees required to wear either positive or negative pressure tight-fitting face-piece respirators. This includes both air-purifying and atmosphere-supplying respirators operating in either a positive or negative pressure mode, but does not include any loose-fitting facepieces.

Must I perform fit testing for workers who voluntarily wear tight-fitting facepiece respirators?

No. If an employee chooses to wear a tight-fitting facepiece respirator (including a negative pressure air-purifying respirator or a filtering facepiece (dust mask)) in a worksite environment where such equipment is not required, you are not required to conduct fit testing.

(f)(2) When fit testing must be conducted: general requirements

You must ensure that fit testing is conducted for all employees required to wear tight-fitting facepiece respirators as follows:

- Prior to initial use.
- Whenever an employee switches to a different tight-fitting facepiece respirator (for example, a different size, make or model).
- At least annually.

(f)(3) When fit testing must be conducted: changes in the respirator wearer's physical condition

You must ensure that an additional fit test is conducted if an employee experiences a change in physical condition that could affect the seal on a tight-fitting facepiece respirator. This requirement is triggered by a physical change:

- Reported by the respirator user.
- Observed by you, a physician or other licensed healthcare professional, the supervisor, or the program administrator.

Physical changes in the employee that might affect the facepiece-to-face seal could include, for example, an obvious change in body weight, facial scarring, extensive dental work, or cosmetic surgery.

(f)(4) When fit testing must be conducted: unacceptable fit as determined by an employee after fit testing

If, after fit testing, an employee reports that his or her respirator does not fit properly, you must allow the employee a reasonable opportunity to select a different tight-fitting facepiece respirator.

After another respirator is selected, you must conduct a new fit test on the employee's replacement equipment.

An employee might determine that the facepiece does not establish an effective facepiece-to-face seal, for example, upon detecting a worksite contaminant while wearing the respirator with new cartridges, or an employee might hear or feel air leaking around the facepiece-to-face seal. The employee's determination also can be based on factors unrelated to the particular worksite. For example, the employee might find that he or she can not wear the respirator for extended periods without experiencing irritation or pain.

(f)(5) Fit testing procedures: general fit testing procedures

You must ensure that all fit testing conducted for employees required to wear tight-fitting facepiece respirators follows the OSHA-approved protocols.

Detailed protocols for qualitative and quantitative fit testing are provided as part of the standard at *Appendix A*. Attachment 3 provides a copy of the standard. These protocols specify that you must have on hand during fit testing all types and sizes of respirators that are available for use at the worksite. This allows you to ensure that each employee is tested with the same type of respirator (make, model, style, and size) that he or she will wear at the worksite.

(f)(6) Limitation on use of qualitative fit testing

The table at the end of this chapter summarizes acceptable means of fit testing (QLFT and QNFT) for different types of respirators. For more information, consult OSHA's website at http://www.osha.gov.

Qualitative fit tests (QLFT) are those using Bitrex, Saccharin, Irritant smoke, or Isoamyl acetate as challenge agents.

QLFT may be used to fit test all positive pressure respirators (air-supplying and PAPRs). Your use of qualitative fit testing on negative pressure air-purifying respirators is limited to those that must achieve a fit factor of 100 or less. Dividing the fit factor of 100 by a standard safety factor of 10 indicates that the negative pressure air-purifying respirators that have successfully completed a qualitative fit test can be relied on to reduce an employee's exposure by a protection factor of 10. The safety factor of 10 is used because protection factors that employees achieve at work sites tend to be much lower than the fit factors achieved during fit testing.

In practice, this means that any negative pressure air-purifying respirator (APR) may be qualitatively fit tested if the APR is to be used in workplace atmos-pheres where the level of the hazardous contaminant is

10 times or less than the permissible exposure limit (PEL) and lower than the level that is immediately dangerous to life or health (IDLH). For example, if the PEL for a specific workplace contaminant is 5 ppm, you could use a qualitative fit test to fit test a negative pressure APR to be used in the workplace at exposure levels up to 50 ppm (ten times the PEL or less). Both half facepiece APRs and full facepiece APRs may be qualitatively fit tested if they are to be worn in work areas where the concentration of contaminant is no more than ten times the PEL. If a full facepiece APR is to be used in atmospheres with levels of contamination greater than ten (10) times the PEL, a quantitative fit test must be used. *(See section (f)(7).)*

The quantitative fit tests are:

- The Portacount
- CNP
- CNP REDON

(f)(7) Use of quantitative fit testing

If quantitative testing is used to fit test a tight-fitting facepiece respirator, respirator fit is not acceptable unless:

- For a half or quarter facepiece: The fit factor achieved in the test is greater than or equal to 100.
- For a full facepiece: The fit factor achieved in the test is greater than or equal to 500.

The following quantitative fit testing procedures (QNFT) have been demonstrated to be acceptable: Portacount, Controlled Negative Pressure (CNP), and Controlled Negative Pressure REDON (CNP REDON).

When using a QNFT, a non-hazardous test aerosol is generated and appropriate instrumentation measures the respirator fit.

(f)(8) Fit testing for atmosphere-supplying and powered air-purifying respirators

You must ensure that all fit testing conducted for employees issued tight-fitting atmosphere-supplying respirators and powered air-purifying respirators is conducted in the negative pressure mode, even if the respirator will be used with positive pressure. This is because it is difficult outside of a laboratory test situation to accurately perform fit testing on positive pressure respirators.

In what circumstances might an atmosphere-supplying or powered air-purifying respirator (PAPR) perform like a negative pressure respirator?

If the blower component of a PAPR loses power because it is turned off or the batteries run out, the respirator will become a negative pressure respirator.

Also, powered air-purifying respirators and self-contained breathing apparatus units can perform like negative pressure respirators when the user increases his or her inhalation rate during heavy work. The increased inhalation rate can result in negative pressure spikes inside the facepiece that are greater than the positive pressure of the air being supplied. This is called "overbreathing the respirator." Therefore, positive air flow alone cannot be counted on to prevent the leakage that can occur with a poorly fitting facepiece.

You can conduct qualitative or quantitative fit testing of tight-fitting atmosphere-supplying respirators and powered air-purifying respirators according to the following requirements.

Qualitative fit testing. To conduct qualitative fit testing on an atmosphere-supplying respirator, you must do one of the following:

- Temporarily convert the user's actual facepiece into a negative pressure respirator by installing the appropriate filters. If you are not sure how to do this, check with the respirator manufacturer or your supplier;
- Use an identical negative pressure facepiece (size, make, model); or
- You can conduct qualitative fit testing on a powered air-purifying respirator by simply turning off the blower.

Quantitative fit testing. To conduct quantitative fit testing on an atmosphere-supplying respirator, you must temporarily or permanently install a sampling probe or adaptor inside the facepiece.

In preparation for testing, you should contact the respirator manufacturer or supplier for information on

Occupational Safety and Health Administration

whether a sampling adapter can be temporarily installed in the facepiece.

Any modifications made to a respirator for testing purposes must be removed before use.

If temporary modifications cannot be made, you will need to permanently convert the facepiece to allow for testing. If you permanently convert the facepiece – for example, by drilling a hole in the respirator facepiece to insert the probe – you cannot repair the hole and put the respirator back in service. Once a hole is drilled in the facepiece, the respirator can only be used for fit testing purposes. It is no longer approved for workplace use.

What is the CNP REDON Fit Test?

The CNP REDON protocol requires the performance of three different test exercises followed by two redonnings of the respirator, while the CNP protocol approved previously by OSHA specifies eight test exercises, including one redonning of the respirator. In addition to amending the standard to include the CNP REDON protocol, this rulemaking made several editorial and non-substantive technical revisions to the Standard associated with the CNP REDON protocol and the previously approved CNP protocol.

This additional quantitative fit testing protocol, the controlled negative pressure (CNP) REDON fit testing protocol, is now included in *Appendix A of the final Respiratory Protection standard. (See Attachment 3 at page 67.)* The protocol affects, in addition to general industry, OSHA respiratory protection standards for shipyard employment and construction.

Are any new fit test methods being developed?

Yes, OSHA approved a new fit test, see Attachment 3 at page 67 of the guide.

The Respiratory Protection standard included a provision for the development of new, faster, less costly fit tests. *Part II of Appendix A of the Respiratory Protection standard,* at Attachment 3 of this guide, specifies, in part, the procedure individuals must follow to submit new fit testing protocols for the Agency's consideration. The criteria OSHA uses for determining whether to propose adding a fit testing protocol to the Respiratory Protection standard include: (1) A test report prepared by an independent government research laboratory (e.g., Lawrence Livermore National Laboratory (LLNL), Los Alamos National Laboratory (LANL), the National Institute for Standards and Technology) stating that the laboratory tested the protocol and found it to be accurate and reliable; (2) an article published in a peer-reviewed industrial hygiene

journal describing the protocol, and explaining how test data support the accuracy and reliability of the protocol. When a protocol meets one of these criteria, the Agency conducts a notice-and-comment rulemaking under *Section 6(b)(7) of the OSH Act of 1970 (29 U.S.C. 655).* The purpose of this provision was to allow for the development of new technology for fit tests, allowing for faster and better fit test methods, as well as new fit test choices for employers. As OSHA noted in the proposal, the CNP REDON protocol met the second of these criteria (68 FR 33887; June 6, 2003).

Acceptable Fit Testing Methods

Respirator	QNFT	QLFT
Half Face, Negative Pressure, APR (<100 fit factor)	Yes	Yes
Full face, Negative Pressure, APR (<100 fit factor) used in atmospheres up to 10 times the PEL	Yes	Yes
Full face, Negative Pressure, APR (>100 fit factor)	Yes	No
PAPR	Yes	Yes
Supplied-Air Respirators (SAR), or SCBA used in Negative Pressure (Demand Mode) (>100 fit factor)	Yes	No
SCBA - Structural Fire Fighting, Positive Pressure	Yes	Yes
SCBA/SAR - IDLH, Positive Pressure	Yes	Yes
Mouthbit Respirators	Fit Testing Not Required	
Loose-fitting Respirators (e.g., hoods, helmets)	Fit Testing Not Required	

Examples of respirators that require fit testing (tight-fitting) are depicted on following pages. In cases in which elastomeric facepieces are used, remember that elastomeric facepieces are made from natural or synthetic rubber or silicone; EPDM is an acronym for a specific type of rubber, that is, Ethylene propylene diene M-class rubber.

Air-purifying respirators

Air-purifying respirators, which remove contaminants from the air.

Half mask Filtering Facepiece Dust mask
APF=10
Needs to be fit tested

Half mask Elastomeric Respirator
APF=10
Needs to be fit tested

Full Facepiece Elastomeric Respirator
APF=50
Needs to be fit tested

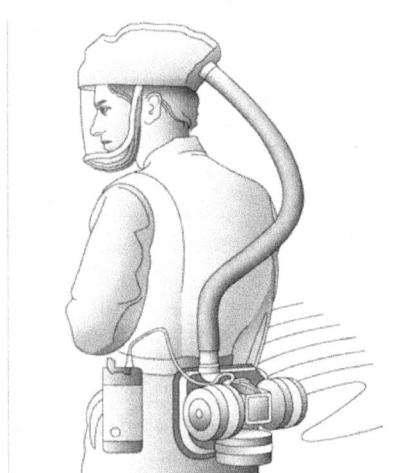

Loose-Fitting Powered Air-Purifying Respirator (PAPR)
APF=25

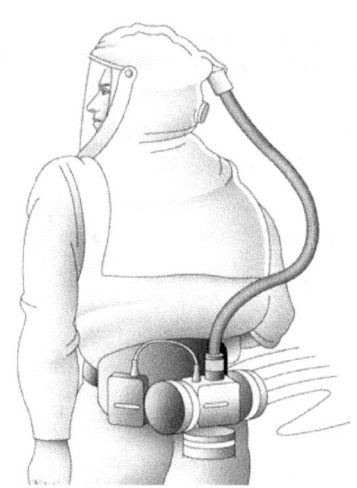

Hooded Powered Air-Purifying Respirator (PAPR)
APF=25 (1,000)*

* Footnote 4 of the APF Table.

Occupational Safety and Health Administration

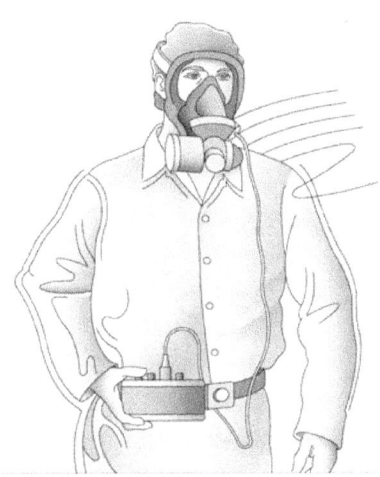
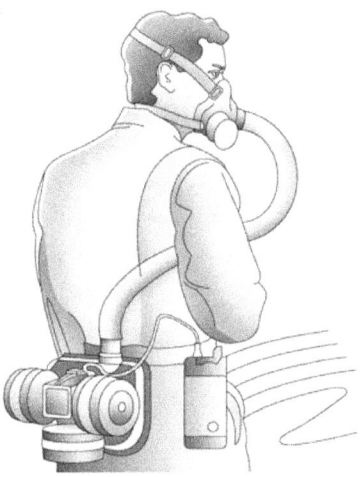

**Tight-Fitting Full Facepiece
Powered Air-Purifying Respirator
(PAPR)**
APF= 1,000
Needs to be fit tested

**Tight-Fitting Half Facepiece
Powered Air-Purifying Respirator
(PAPR)**
APF= 50
Needs to be fit tested

Atmosphere-supplying respirators

Atmosphere-supplying respirators, which provide clean air from an uncontaminated source.

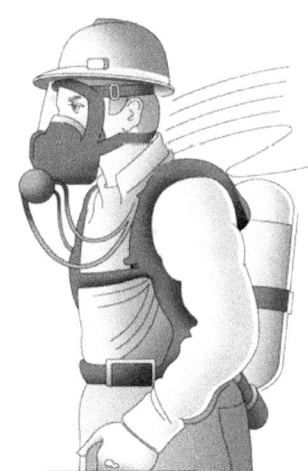
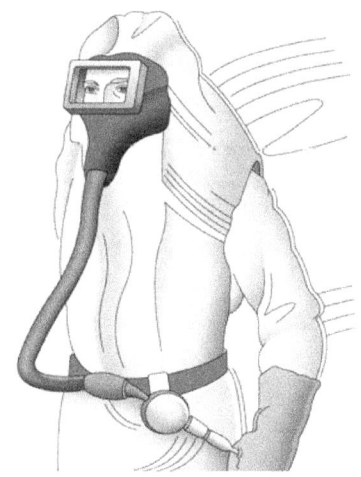

**Tight-fitting Self-Contained
Breathing Apparatus (SCBA)
pressure-demand mode**
APF=10,000
demand mode
APF=50
Needs to be fit tested

**Tight-fitting Abrasive Blasting
Respirator Continuous flow**
APF=25/1,000*
SAR Full Facepiece
Needs to be fit tested

**Tight-fitting Atmosphere-Supplying
Respirator with an auxiliary escape
bottle**
APF=10,000 in escape mode only;
otherwise APF=1,000
Full facepiece
Needs to be fit tested

* Footnote 4 of the APF Table.

Filtering facepiece (N95) respirators, surgical (N95) respirators, and surgical masks

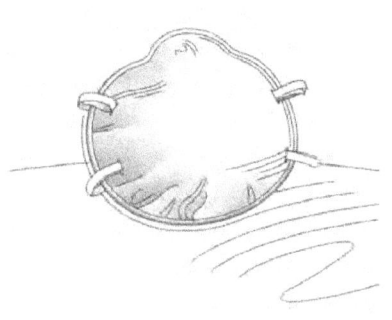  

Filtering facepiece (N95) surgical mask   **Surgical (N95) respirator**   **Surgical mask**

Respirators are designed to reduce a worker's exposure to airborne contaminants. Respirators come in various sizes and must be individually selected to fit the wearer's face and to provide a tight seal. A proper seal between the user's face and the respirator forces the inhaled air through the respirator's filter material and not through gaps between the face and the respirator. Both the filtering facepiece (N95) respirators and the surgical (N95) respirators must be fit tested to ensure that a proper seal exists between the employee's face and the respirator. Both of the respirators provide protection from exposures to airborne influenza flu viruses. Whenever respirators are required by employees (e.g., N95 and Surgical N95 respirators), they must be NIOSH-certified and selected and used in compliance with OSHA's Respiratory Protection standard.

Surgical masks and surgical (N95) respirators are used as a physical barrier to protect the user from hazards, such as large droplets of: splashes or sprays of human and animal blood; any unfixed tissue, organs, tissue and organ cultures (including those from experimental animals); other secretions that are visibly contaminated with blood; and, all body fluids in situations where it is difficult or impossible to differentiate between body fluids. Surgical masks, by themselves, are not designed to seal tightly against the user's face and are not subject to fit testing. Surgical masks are not designed or certified to prevent the inhalation of small airborne particles that are not visible to the naked eye but may still be capable of causing infection.

OSHA®
Occupational Safety and
Health Administration

Section (g): Use of respirators

As part of your written program, you must establish and implement procedures for the proper use of respirators in both routine jobs and emergencies. Specific procedures are required to:

• Prevent leaks in the respirator facepiece seal.

• Prevent employees from removing respirators in hazardous environments.

• Ensure that respirators operate effectively throughout the work shift.

• Protect employees entering IDLH atmospheres and interior structural firefighting situations.

(g)(1) Preventing leaks in the facepiece seal

Facepiece seals and valves are important in tight-fitting respirators. Tight-fitting respirators should be able to provide a complete seal to the face. If there is a leak in the seal of a tight-fitting respirator or valve, then the respirator cannot effectively reduce the wearer's exposures to respiratory hazards. You must be sure that nothing interferes with the seal of the respirator to the employee's face or with the valves. You must also ensure that employees check the seal of a tight-fitting respirator by conducting a user seal check each time the employee dons the respirator.

Conditions that can interfere with the seal or valve are specified in the standard and include:

• Facial hair;

• Facial scars;

• Jewelry or headgear that projects under the facepiece seal;

• Missing dentures; and

• Corrective glasses or goggles or other protective equipment such as:

  - Face shields

  - Protective clothing

  - Helmets

  - Eyeglass insert or spectacle kits

Employees may use this equipment with tight-fitting respirators if you ensure that the equipment is worn in a way that:

• Does not interfere with the face-to-facepiece seal.

• Does not distort the employee's vision.

• Does not cause physical harm to the employee (e.g., if the eyeglass insert did not fit properly so that the tight fit of the respirator caused the insert to press against his or her forehead, eyes, or temples).

You must make sure that the employee's eyewear does not interfere with the respirator seal, or that the worker has to remove the eyewear altogether.

What if an employee has a condition that does not interfere with the face-to-facepiece seal?

As long as the condition does not interfere with the function of the respirator valves, then the employee can wear a tight-fitting respirator, provided that the employee has no other conditions that interfere with the face-to-facepiece seal or valve. For example, a mustache may not interfere with the facepiece seal but may interfere with the valve function.

Do these restrictions apply to all types of respirators?

The restrictions for facial hair and other conditions apply ONLY to tight-fitting respirators. Several respiratory protection alternatives, such as loose-fitting hoods or helmets, are available to accommodate employees with facial hair or with other conditions that might interfere with the seal of the facepiece to the face of the user.

Can employeess wear contact lenses?

Yes, contact lenses can be safely worn with respirators.

What is a user seal check?

You must be sure that employees perform user seal checks each time they put on a tight-fitting respirator. User seal checks are a quick and easy way for employees to verify that they have put on their respirators correctly and that the respirators are working properly.

To conduct a user seal check, the employee must follow either the procedures for a user seal check that are contained in *Appendix B-1 to § 1910.134: User Seal Check Procedures (Mandatory),* or equally effective procedures that the respirator manufacturer recommends for conducting a user seal check. A copy of the standard is in Attachment 3 of this guide.

How are user seal checks conducted?

To conduct a user seal check, the employee performs a negative or positive pressure fit check.

For the negative pressure check, the employee:

- covers the respirator inlets (cartridges, canisters, or seals)

- gently inhales, and

- holds breath for 10 seconds.

The facepiece should collapse on the worker's face and remain collapsed.

For the positive pressure check, the worker:

- covers the respirator exhalation valve(s), and

- exhales.

The facepiece should hold the positive pressure for a few seconds. During this time, the employee should not hear or feel the air leaking out of the face-to-face-piece seal. *Appendix B-1 of the Respiratory Protection standard* provides detailed instructions on how to conduct the user seal check. Attachment 3 of this guide provides a copy of the standard.

The manufacturer's recommended procedures for checking the facepiece seal may be used if the employer demonstrates that the manufacturer's procedures are as effective as those described in *Appendix B-1 of the Respiratory Protection standard* (i.e., these procedures are effective in identifying respirators that fit poorly when put on or adjusted).

Can a user seal check be used as a substitute for a qualitative fit test?

No, a user seal check is *not* a substitute for a qualitative fit test. Fit testing is a more rigorous procedure that is used to determine whether the respirator fits the face of the employee. Section (f) of this Compliance Guide contains a complete discussion on respirator fit testing. *(See fit testing in Appendix A of the standard; See user seal check in Appendix B-1 of the standard.)* A copy of the standard is provided in Attachment 3 of this guide.

How can employers ensure that workers perform user seal checks?

A major purpose of the standard is to make sure that the fit and performance of the respirator is not compromised. You must take actions that will result in safe work practices. Examples of these actions include:

- Providing training to workers

- Routinely observing work practices

- Routinely monitoring site conditions

- Consulting workers

Example of a worker performing a user seal check on a half mask elastomeric air-purifying respirator

(g)(2) Continuing respirator effectiveness

You must be aware of conditions in work areas where employees are using respirators. You must also allow employees to leave the respirator use area to perform any activity that involves removing or adjusting a respirator facepiece, or if there is any indication that a respirator may not be fully effective. If there is any indication that they are not functioning properly, you must repair or discard and replace respirators before allowing employees to return to an area in which respirator use is required.

Workplace conditions include the following:

- The level of the contaminant in relation to the APF

- The size and configuration of the workspace

- Ease of employee communication

- Ease or difficulty of the work or rate of activity

- The type of workplace tasks and proximity to the source of contamination, e.g., cutting wood on a band saw would differ from hand polishing a wood veneer on furniture.

- Workplace conditions such as temperature and humidity or the location and movement of other personnel and equipment.

How can I conduct appropriate surveillance?

"Appropriate surveillance" means that you must routinely look for any changes that may affect the effectiveness of a respirator. You must look for changes in the work area, such as changes in work tasks or processes, that can result in changes in the hazard or the time period of exposure, or that put the employee in closer proximity to the hazard. Another change might be the addition of new machinery that would cause an employee to exert more energy and breathe harder.

By "appropriate surveillance" OSHA means that you must routinely observe employees as they work while wearing respirators. By observing respirator use under actual workplace conditions, you can determine:

- Whether other protective equipment is interfering with respirator use.

- Whether a change in working conditions may result in exposure to new contaminants or an increase in contaminant exposure.

- Whether employees are experiencing discomfort, such as skin irritation or breakthrough of contaminants through cartridges and canisters.

If any of these conditions exist, you must make adjustments – such as providing a more protective respirator or a different size or style of respirator, or altering work practices to reduce the stress on

employees – to ensure that employees continue to receive adequate respiratory protection.

When must employees leave the exposure areas to maintain the integrity of their respirators?

To maintain their respirators, employees may, from time to time, need to leave the area where respirator use is required and go to a safe area free of respiratory hazards and contaminants.

Employees must leave the respirator use area:

- If the employee needs to wash his or her face or the respirator facepiece to prevent eye or skin irritation associated with respirator use.

- If the employee detects vapor or gas breakthrough (that is, the cartridge or canister is saturated with contaminant and needs to be changed).

- If the employee notices that the facepiece is leaking.

- If the employee observes a change in breathing resistance (that is, the filter is full of dust or other particles and needs to be changed).

- If the respirator or parts of the respirator, such as valves or straps, are not working properly and need to be replaced.

Employees need a "safe area" in the workplace where they can safely remove their respirators to wash or conduct the maintenance necessary to ensure the respirator's adequate operation. Through training and supervision, employees must know the conditions of respirator use that require them to leave the exposure areas and go to a safe area.

Where does the safe area need to be located?

The safe area must be located in a place that is free of respiratory hazards or contamination. As long as these conditions are met, the safe area can be in a location that minimizes interruptions to work flow.

How often do respirators need to be replaced or repaired?

There is no required replacement schedule for respirators in general. However, damaged respirators cannot properly protect workers. Respirators need to be replaced or repaired when one or more of their components is missing, damaged, or visibly deteriorated.

(g)(3) Procedures for Immediately Dangerous to Life or Health atmospheres and for interior structural firefighting

This section of the Respiratory Protection standard contains requirements for respirator use in IDLH environments. The standard defines IDLH as "an atmosphere that poses an immediate threat to life, would cause irreversible adverse health effects, or would impair an individual's ability to escape from a dangerous atmosphere." (See Section (d) of this guide or *paragraphs (g)(3)-(4)* of the standard.)

The provisions of *paragraph (g)(3)* of the Respiratory Protection standard are requirements for respirator use in all IDLH atmospheres. *Paragraph (g)(4)* contains additional requirements applicable only to the extra-hazardous environments encountered during "interior structural fire fighting." Information about "interior structural fire fighting" is explained further in section (g)(4) of the guide. OSHA considers interior structural firefighting environments to be IDLH environments. These two paragraphs, *((g)(3) and (g)(4))*, deal with requirements for standby personnel and the respirator users inside the IDLH atmosphere. The standard requires standby personnel when employees use respirators in IDLH environments. These two provisions ensure that adequate rescue capability exists in case of respirator failure or some other emergency inside the IDLH environment.

Who are standby personnel?

Standby personnel are firefighters who remain outside the IDLH atmosphere. They must be available, trained, and equipped to assist respirator users inside the IDLH atmosphere, and to provide effective emergency rescue, when needed.

You must be sure that standby personnel maintain visual, voice, or signal line communication with the employees in the IDLH environment. Standby personnel may use radios to communicate with workers inside the IDLH environment. You must be sure that standby personnel notify you or your designated representative before entering the IDLH atmosphere. Once notified, you must provide necessary assistance appropriate to the situation.

When do I need to have more than one standby person located outside the IDLH environment?

A single standby person is adequate if an IDLH environment is well characterized and controlled, and if one person can easily maintain communication with all employees in the IDLH environment. Two stand-by personnel are required for interior structural firefighting. An IDLH atmosphere is "well characterized" if it has been monitored and the results of the monitoring have been analyzed, or if it has been through a process-hazard analysis. (Chemical plants conduct comprehensive process-hazard analyses as required by OSHA's Process Safety Management standard [29 CFR 1910.119] to determine which process units pose IDLH hazards.)

Often, only one respirator user at a time is exposed to an IDLH atmosphere, and a single standby person can easily monitor that employee's status. Even in situations where more than one respirator user is inside an IDLH environment, a single standby person can often provide adequate communication and support. For example, one standby person can easily communicate with more than one employee working inside a small pump room or shed.

More than one standby person may be required for other situations. For example, to clean and paint the inside of a multi-level, multi-portal water tower, a process that often generates a deadly atmosphere as a result of cleaning solutions and paint-solvent vapors, employees often enter the tower through different portals to work on different levels. In such a situation, there will be a need for good communication at each entry portal, and more than one standby person would be needed to maintain adequate communication and accessibility (See also 29 CFR 1910.146, Confined Spaces).

When must standby personnel maintain communication with employees in the IDLH atmosphere?

Standby personnel must maintain communication with employees in the IDLH atmosphere at all times. Voice, visual, or hand signal line communication must be continuously maintained between the employee(s) in the IDLH environment and the standby person. Because IDLH conditions present the potential for serious injury or death, there is little margin for error in an IDLH environment. Equipment malfunction in an IDLH environment can swiftly disable employees, prevent them from leaving the environment, and lead to severe injury or death. For this reason, close communication between standby personnel and respirator users in the IDLH environment is critical.

When is radio communication acceptable?

Standby personnel must be in visual, voice, or signal-line communication with the employees inside the IDLH environment. However, standby personnel may communicate by two-way radio (intrinsically safe) with employees inside the IDLH environment, if use of visual, voice, or signal-line communication is not feasible. A standby employee should have a telephone or radio to summon additional help, and should not enter an IDLH environment for rescue until help arrives. The standby person also must be able to assist in providing or obtaining effective emergency assistance to employees inside the IDLH environment. In interior structural firefighting situations, firefighters inside the burning structure may communicate with one another by two-way radio, but they must also remain in visual or voice contact with each other.

Is voice communication the only acceptable method for employees in the IDLH environment and standby personnel to communicate with one another?

No, communication can be in the form of signal lines. It is advisable to have several means of communication systems available, in the event that one form of communication fails.

What is appropriate training and equipment for the standby personnel?

You must train the standby personnel to:

- Provide effective emergency rescue; and

- Notify you or your designated representative before the standby personnel enter the IDLH atmosphere to attempt an emergency rescue.

You must equip your standby personnel with the following:

- Pressure demand or other positive pressure SCBAs, or a pressure demand or other positive pressure supplied-air respirator with auxiliary SCBA; and

- Either appropriate retrieval equipment for removing the employees inside the IDLH atmosphere where retrieval equipment would contribute to the rescue of the employees inside the IDLH atmosphere and would not increase the overall risk resulting from entry; or

- Equivalent means for rescue where retrieval equipment could increase the overall risk resulting from entry.

- For employees involved in interior structural fire-fighting, standby personnel must be equipped with SCBAs.

Rescue personnel must be properly trained and protected before they enter the IDLH environment. The Hazardous Waste Operations and Emergency Response standard (29 CFR 1910.120) and the Permit-Required Confined Spaces standard (29 CFR 1910.146) provide guidance on the training and protective equipment that is required. Situations exist in which retrieval lines (harnesses, wristlets, anklets) may pose an entanglement problem, especially in areas in which air lines or electrical cords are present in the work areas in which the IDLH atmosphere occurs. Most of the time, however, rescue with retrieval equipment is effective, and much safer for the rescuers because the standby personnel do not have to enter the IDLH atmosphere.

If there is an emergency, can the standby provide immediate rescue assistance?

Your standby personnel must inform either you or your designated representative before attempting emergency rescue within an IDLH environment. Your designated representative may be a properly trained employee or response team, or local firefighting and emergency rescue personnel. In any case, proper arrangements and procedures must be in place before you can allow your employees to enter an IDLH environment. Once notified, you must provide necessary assistance appropriate to the situation.

This provision of the standard ensures that you know when an emergency has occurred so that you or your designated representative can send in immediate additional assistance to help in the rescue.

When should standby personnel enter the IDLH environment?

Under most circumstances, standby personnel should not enter the IDLH environment until you or your designated representative has responded to the notification acknowledging that an emergency exists, that rescue personnel are entering the IDLH environment, and that emergency response units are on their way to provide additional assistance. You must provide standby personnel (rescuers) with proper respiratory equipment, and you must train and prepare your standby personnel to facilitate rescue attempts.

This notification provision does not require that standby employees should wait indefinitely for you or your authorized designee to respond to notification before entering the IDLH atmosphere when your employees inside are in danger and standby personnel are appropriately trained and equipped to provide assistance. In the majority of cases, however, rescuers should not enter the IDLH environment until receiving some response from you (i.e., you or your designated representative should know that the rescuers are entering and emergency response units should be on their way to the incident).

How must I provide appropriate assistance in emergencies?

Once you or your designated representative has been notified, you or your representative must provide the necessary assistance appropriate for the situation. You must make sure that:

- Rescue operations are carried out appropriately

- Rescuers are provided with proper respiratory equipment

- Designated employees are adequately prepared to conduct rescue attempts

You may not always need to send standby personnel into the hazardous atmosphere. In some cases, the employee within the IDLH environment will be able to get out on his or her own, or retrieval equipment may enable rescuers to retrieve the employee without entering the hazardous atmosphere. In these instances, you must be prepared to provide employees inside IDLH atmospheres and standby personnel employees with emergency medical treatment.

You should consult OSHA's rules on confined spaces (29 CFR 1910.146) and on hazardous waste operations and emergency response (29 CFR 1910.120) for other provisions that may apply to IDLH environments.

(g)(4) Procedures for interior structural firefighting

This portion of the standard applies to employees engaged in interior structural firefighting only. Federal OSHA does not cover public employees such as firefighters. However, public employees are covered by the State OSHA programs in the 27 states that operate their own state programs.

What is interior structural firefighting?

Interior structural firefighting is firefighting to control or extinguish a fire in an advanced stage of burning inside a building. Because the fire is producing large amounts of smoke, heat, and toxic products of combustion, exposure of firefighters is extremely hazardous and the environment is considered IDLH.

For interior structural firefighting, you must have two employees enter the IDLH atmosphere and remain in visual or voice contact with one another at all times. You must also have two standby personnel located outside the IDLH atmosphere (two-in, two-out); all employees engaged in interior structural firefighting must use SCBAs.

Are all firefighters engaged in interior structural firefighting covered by the standard?

Yes, when OSHA's Respiratory Protection standard is applied to private-sector employees engaged in firefighting covered under Section 19 of the Occupational Safety and Health Act. These employees include those working in industrial fire brigades and private incorporated fire companies. Federal agencies must comply with the Respiratory Protection standard or an equally stringent standard, pursuant to Executive Order 12196 and 29 CFR 1960.17, covered under Section 6 of the Occupational Safety and Health Act (with a general exemption for military personnel and operations).

There are 27 states and territories that enforce occupational safety and health requirements. In these states and territories, enforcement of occupational safety and health requirements is by the State agency responsible for the OSHA-approved state plan. These states are required to extend their coverage to state and local government employees, including public sector

firefighters, who are not otherwise covered by Federal OSHA. The states and territories operating OSHA-approved state plans are: Alaska, Arizona, California, Hawaii, Indiana, Iowa, Kentucky, Maryland, Michigan, Minnesota, Nevada, New Mexico, North Carolina, Oregon, Puerto Rico, South Carolina, Tennessee, Utah, Vermont, Virginia, Washington, and Wyoming. Connecticut, New Jersey, New York, and the Virgin Islands operate OSHA-approved state plans that apply to state and local government employees only.

Coverage of volunteer firefighters varies by State and depends on State law. State and local government employees in states that do not operate OSHA-approved state plans are not covered by these requirements, unless the requirements are voluntarily adopted for local applicability.

What additional requirements apply to interior structural firefighting?

In addition to the requirements for all IDLH atmospheres, if your employees are involved in interior structural firefighting, you must be certain that:

*   At least two employees enter the IDLH atmosphere and remain in visual or voice contact with one another at all times and at least two employees are located outside the IDLH atmosphere, namely the "two in, two out" policy.

*   All employees engaged in interior structural firefighting use SCBAs.

*   Although two individuals must always be located outside the IDLH atmosphere, one may be assigned to an additional role, such as incident command, pump operations, or operator of the fire apparatus – so long as this individual is able to perform assistance or rescue activities without jeopardizing the safety or health of any firefighter working at the incident. Any assignment of additional duties to the second firefighter must be weighed against the potential for the additional duties to interfere with assistance or rescue activities.

Must firefighters wait until four employees are assembled before attempting to rescue victims inside the burning structure?

No, there is an explicit exemption in the Respiratory Protection standard that states that if life is in jeopardy the "two-in, two-out" requirement is waived. The incident commander and the firefighters at the scene must decide whether the risks posed by entering the interior structural fire before at least four firefighters have assembled is outweighed by the need to rescue a victim whose life may be at risk.

Section (h): Maintenance and care of respirators

You must provide respirator users with equipment that is clean, sanitary, and in good working order. To accomplish this you must have a system of respirator care and maintenance as a component of your respiratory protection program. Regular care and maintenance is important to ensure that the equipment functions as designed and protects the user from the threat of illness or death.

Your system of respirator care and maintenance must provide for:

- cleaning and disinfection procedures
- proper storage
- regular inspections
- repair methods

(h)(1) Cleaning and disinfecting

Respirator equipment must be regularly cleaned and disinfected according to specified procedures (*See Appendix B-2* of the standard; a copy of the standard is provided at Attachment 3 of this guide) or according to manufacturer specifications that are of equivalent effectiveness.

Cleaning and disinfection procedures are divided into the following:

- Disassembly of components
- Cleaning and disinfecting
- Rinsing, drying and reassembly
- Testing

How often must respirators be cleaned and disinfected?

The frequency of cleaning and disinfecting or sanitizing respirators will depend in part on whether your employees share the equipment or are issued respirators for their exclusive use. Worksite conditions also dictate cleaning frequency; e.g., working in a dirty environment will require that the respirator facepiece, in particular, be cleaned more frequently. The frequency must be noted in your written respiratory protection plan.

At a minimum:

If a respirator is...

- issued for the exclusive use of an individual employee, the equipment must be cleaned and disinfected as often as necessary to be maintained in clean and sanitary condition.

- used by more than one employee, the equipment must be cleaned and disinfected before being used by different individuals.

- maintained for use in emergencies, testing, and training exercises, the equipment must be cleaned and disinfected *after* each use.

CHECKLIST FOR PROPER USE OF RESPIRATORS

√ Check your facility to be certain that:

❑ Employees using tight-fitting respirators have no conditions, such as facial hair, that would interfere with a face-to-facepiece seal or valve function.

❑ Employees wear corrective glasses, goggles, or other protective equipment in a manner that does not interfere with the face-to-facepiece seal or valve function.

❑ Employees perform user seal checks prior to each use of a tight-fitting respirator.

❑ There are procedures for conducting ongoing surveillance of the work area for conditions that affect respirator effectiveness, and that, when such conditions exist, you take steps to address those situations.

❑ Employees are permitted to leave their work area to conduct respirator maintenance, such as washing the facepiece, or to replace respirator parts.

❑ Employees do not return to their work area until their respirator has been repaired or replaced in the event of a breakthrough, a leak in the facepiece, or a change in breathing resistance.

❑ There are procedures for respirator use in IDLH atmospheres and during interior structural firefighting to ensure that: the appropriate number of standby personnel are deployed; standby personnel and workers in the IDLH environment maintain communication; standby personnel are properly trained, equipped, and prepared; you will be notified when standby personnel enter an IDLH atmosphere; and you will respond appropriately to this notification.

❑ Standby personnel are equipped with a pressure demand or other positive pressure SCBA, or a positive pressure supplied-air respirator with an escape SCBA, and appropriate retrieval equipment or other means for rescue.

❑ Procedures for interior structural firefighting require that: at least two employees enter the IDLH atmosphere and remain in contact with one another at all times; at least two standby personnel are used; and all firefighting employees use SCBAs.

Who is responsible for cleaning and disinfecting respirators?

You may choose the program that best meets the needs of your workplace. For example, you may use a centralized operation where employees receive respirators that have been cleaned, disinfected and repaired by employees assigned to this task. You also may require that each respirator wearer be responsible for cleaning and maintaining his or her own equipment. In either case, you must provide the necessary equipment and supplies and, in addition, you must provide appropriate training and allow on-the-job time for the training and for the cleaning and maintenance of respirators.

(h)(2) Storage

What are the proper storage procedures for respirators?

You must store respirators in a manner that:

- Protects them from contamination, dust, sunlight, extreme temperatures, excessive moisture, damaging chemicals, or other destructive conditions.
- Prevents the facepiece or valves from becoming deformed.
- Follows all storage precautions issued by the respirator manufacturer.

In addition, if a respirator is for emergency use, it must be:

- Kept accessible to the work area, but not in an area that may itself become involved in an emergency and become contaminated or inaccessible.
- Stored in a compartment or cover (e.g., on a fire truck) that is clearly identified as containing emergency equipment.
- Stored according to the manufacturer's instructions.

(h)(3) Inspection

How often must respirators be inspected, and what procedures do I follow?

The frequency of and procedures for inspections depend on whether the respirator is designed for non-emergency, emergency, or escape-only use.

All respirator inspections must include:

- A check of respirator function, tightness of connections, and the condition of the various parts, including, but not limited to the facepiece, head straps, valves, connecting tubes, and cartridges, canisters, or filters. A visual inspection of the respirator may identify parts that may be missing, distorted, blocked, loose, deteriorated, or otherwise interfere with proper performance. *(See (g)(2) of the standard.)*

- A check of elastomeric (rubber) parts for pliability and deterioration.

In addition, inspect:

- **Non-emergency use equipment.** *Before* each use and *during* cleaning and disinfection.

- **Self-contained breathing apparatus (SCBA).** *Monthly*, making sure the air and oxygen cylinders that are available for immediate use are maintained in a fully charged state (i.e., pressure is not below 90% of manufacturer's recommended level). You must also activate the regulator and low pressure warning devices to ensure that they function properly.

- **Emergency use respirators.** *At least monthly,* checking for proper functioning *before and after each use.* When inspecting these types of respirators you must:

  - Document the date of inspection, name or signature of inspector, inspection findings, any remedial action required, and serial number or other identification of the respirator.

  - Retain this information with the respirator, in the storage compartment or inspection report until the next certification. You may use tags or labels to document the inspections.

- **Emergency escape-only equipment.** *Before* being carried into the workplace for use.

The frequency must be noted in your written respiratory protection plan.

(h)(4) Repairs

What do I do if a respirator fails to pass inspection?

If a respirator does not pass inspection, you must remove the respirator from service and discard, repair, or adjust it. Tagging out-of-service respirators is a good means for ensuring that defective respirators are not inadvertently used.

When must I replace or repair respirators?

You must replace or repair respirators that are not working properly. Respirators should not be used if they are defective in any way. You must replace or repair a defective respirator whenever the employee detects vapor or gas breakthrough, changes in breathing resistance, or facepiece leakage, and before allowing the employee to return to the work area where respirator use is required.

Who performs the repair work?

Respirators may be repaired only by an appropriately trained person who must use NIOSH-certified parts

OSHA®
**Occupational Safety and
Health Administration**

that are designed for the particular respirator being repaired.

Valves, regulators, and alarms must be adjusted and repaired only by the manufacturer or a technician trained by the manufacturer.

What are some examples of when a respirator should be removed from service?

- An alarm system is not functioning on an SCBA.

- A respirator strap, buckle, or connection is damaged or missing.

- The mask portion of a respirator is misshapen or degraded and can no longer form a good seal around the user's face.

CHECKLIST FOR RESPIRATOR MAINTENANCE AND CARE

√ Check to make sure that your facility has met the following requirements:

Cleaning and disinfecting:

❑ Respirators are provided that are clean, sanitary, and in good working order.

❑ Respirators are cleaned and disinfected using the procedures specified in *Appendix B-2 of the standard.*

Respirators are cleaned and disinfected:

❑ As often as necessary when issued for the exclusive use of one employee.

❑ Before being worn by different individuals.

❑ After each use for emergency use respirators.

❑ After each use for respirators used for fit testing and training.

Storage:

❑ Respirators are stored to protect them from damage from the elements, and from becoming deformed.

Emergency respirators are stored:

❑ To be accessible to the work area.

❑ In compartments marked as such.

❑ In accord with manufacturer's instructions.

Inspections:

❑ Routine-use respirators are inspected before each use and during cleaning.

❑ SCBAs and emergency respirators are inspected monthly and checked for proper functioning before and after each use.

❑ Emergency escape-only respirators are inspected before being carried into the workplace for use.

Inspections include:

❑ Check of respirator function.

❑ Tightness of connections.

❑ Condition of the facepiece, head straps, valves, cartridges, and other parts.

❑ Condition of elastomeric parts.

For SCBAs, inspections include:

❑ Check that cylinders are fully charged.

❑ Check that regulators function properly.

❑ Check that warning devices function properly.

For emergency use respirators, inspections include:

❑ Certification by documenting the inspection, and by tagging the information either to the respirator or its compartment, or storing it with inspection reports.

Repairs:

❑ Respirators that have failed inspection are taken out of service.

❑ Repairs are made only by trained personnel.

❑ Only NIOSH-certified parts are used.

❑ Reducing and admission valves, regulators and alarms are adjusted or repaired only by the manufacturer or a technician trained by the manufacturer.

Section (i): Breathing air quality and use

This section of the Respiratory Protection standard requires you to provide employees who are wearing atmosphere-supplying respirators with breathing air of high purity. Respirators that supply breathing air are generally used in highly hazardous work environments. It is critical that such respirator systems provide quality breathing air and that the equipment operates reliably.

More broadly, you are required to establish or continue a respiratory protection program that follows performance standards for the operation and maintenance of breathing air compressors, methods for ensuring breathing air quality, and requirements for the quality of purchased breathing air.

The requirements detailed in this section are critical for ensuring the integrity of high purity breathing air for use with respirators, whether the air is delivered in tanks by a supplier or produced on site using a compressor. Also, it is your responsibility to ensure that practices are in place for protecting the quality of breathing air while stored in containers and when being used by employees. These requirements are essential for protecting respirator-wearing employees from exposure to airborne contaminants.

As detailed below, when using atmosphere-supplying respirators you must:

- Provide breathing air that meets certain specifications.

- Develop procedures to ensure the proper use of compressed gas cylinders and air compressors.

- Implement certain precautions to avoid improper use of couplings on airline systems and confusion about breathing air containers.

- Implement certain precautions to prevent exposure to carbon monoxide when using air compressors.

How is breathing air delivered to the respirator user?

Air compressors capture air from the surrounding environment, filter it, remove oil (if necessary), compress it to increase its density, and deliver the air through a system of regulators that brings the air back down to a breathable pressure for the respirator user.

With SCBA units, the pressurized breathing air is transferred from the tank to the respirator user through regulators that decrease the pressure to a level that a human can breathe. Because there is a fixed amount of air in the tank, the user can only rely on it for a given period of time. That time varies based on the size of the tank, the amount of pressure in the tank, and the physical effort required by the respirator user. Use times range from 20 minutes for low pressure tanks (2,500 psi) to 45 minutes for high pressure tanks (4,500 psi) with moderate physical effort.

The air delivered by both types of systems is at slightly greater than atmospheric pressure, which assists in preventing contaminated air from seeping through gaps in the facepiece.

Breathing air that is supplied "on demand" rather than provided constantly to the user, as in a constant flow type device, is able to be used with a large, compressed air cylinder of breathable air or a bank of cylinders set up in cascading fashion. Cascading breathing air assemblies can be designed to provide breathing air from several assemblies. A pressure reducing regulator is supplied to deliver the correct pressure recommended by the respirator manufacturer. Air cascading simply means equalizing the pressure between the cylinder to be refilled and the next lowest supply cylinder. If this process does not get the desired pressure in the small cylinder, the supply cylinder is turned off and the next highest supply cylinder is opened and the pressure allowed to equalize between the two cylinders. A low pressure warning whistle, or bell, is supplied to notify the user that the cascade system has dropped below specified levels. Check valves are installed on each cylinder stem to prevent pressure equalization. These valves also allow the user to independently change cylinders without depressurizing the complete system.

(i)(1) Specifications for breathing air

You must ensure that compressed air, compressed oxygen, liquid air, and liquid oxygen meet certain specifications as outlined below for breathing by employees wearing atmosphere-supplying respirators. Unless you produce your own breathing air from a compressor, you can rely on certificates of analysis from air suppliers to ensure that breathing air meets the required specifications.

Types of Breathing Air

Compressed air is the most common type of breathing-air system used in worksite applications because it is the most convenient and least expensive. Compressed air is provided either through compressed air cylinders or air compressors at relatively high pressures. Regulators are used to ensure that breathing air supplied to respirators is provided at pressures that are safe for employees to breathe.

Other types of breathing air systems include liquid air, compressed oxygen, and liquid oxygen. Liquid air is air that exists in a liquid state, which is achieved by compressing purified air and chilling it to a temperature below the boiling point of its principal components (i.e., nitrogen and oxygen). Compressed oxygen systems are used in limited applications because they present a significant fire hazard. Liquid oxygen is quite expensive and also presents a significant fire hazard. It is generally used only in very specialized applications.

(i)(1)(i) Compressed and liquid oxygen

Such forms of compressed oxygen must meet the U.S. Pharmacopeia requirements for medical or breathing oxygen.

(i)(1)(ii) Compressed breathing air

Any compressed breathing air must meet at least the requirements for Grade D breathing air described in "Compressed Gas Association Commodity

Occupational Safety and Health Administration

Specification for Air" (CGA G-7.1-1989). This specification requires that:

(A) Oxygen content in compressed breathing air must be 19.5 to 23.5 percent of the total volume of air.

(B) Condensed hydrocarbon content in compressed breathing air must be 5 milligrams (mg) per each cubic meter (m^3) of air or less.

(C) Carbon monoxide content in compressed breathing air must be 10 parts per million (ppm) or less.

(D) Carbon dioxide content in compressed breathing air must be 1,000 ppm or less.

(E) There must be a lack of any noticeable odor from the compressed breathing air.

(i)(2)&(3) Oxygen use

Explosion/fire hazard from compressor oil and grease. You must prohibit employees from using compressed oxygen in respirators that have previously been used with compressed air. The reason for this prohibition is that oil and grease can be introduced into respirator airlines used for compressed air, posing a danger of fire or explosion from the high pressure oxygen coming in contact with the oil or grease. Airline systems contain inline filters for capturing impurities so that the respirator user will not inhale the oil or grease.

Explosion/fire hazard from high concentration oxygen. You must ensure that employees use oxygen concentrations greater than 23.5 percent only with equipment designed specifically for oxygen service and distribution. Such equipment is specifically designed to minimize the risk of fire or explosion posed by the high concentration of oxygen.

(i)(4) Cylinder use

You must ensure that cylinders used with atmosphere-supplying respirators meet the following requirements:

- Cylinders of breathing air must be tested and maintained according to Department of Transportation (DOT) Shipping Container Specification Regulations (49 CFR Parts 173 and 178), which include provisions for the construction, testing, and maintenance of cylinders. These steps are necessary to prevent explosions that can result from a rupture in a breathing air cylinder under high pressure. (Additional guidance is available in 29 CFR 1910.101(b), which includes provisions for in-plant handling and storage of compressed gas cylinders.)

- Cylinders of purchased breathing air must be accompanied by a certificate from the supplier indicating that the contents of each cylinder have been tested and found to meet the criteria for Grade

D breathing air. This certification will provide you with a reasonable assurance that the breathing air supplied to your employees is safe.

- Cylinder contents must have a moisture level that does not exceed a dew point of minus 50° Fahrenheit (F) (minus 45.6° Celsius [C]) at 1 atmosphere pressure. (Dew point refers to the temperature at which the air is saturated with moisture.) This requirement prevents respirator valves from freezing when excess moisture accumulates on the valves, which can cause blockages in the flow of breathing air. You should verify with the supplier that the breathing air meets this requirement.

(i)(5)-(7) Compressor use

You must ensure that compressors used with atmosphere-supplying respirators provide breathing air according to the following requirements:

(i)(5)(i) Location of compressor during use

The location of an air compressor during use is very important to maintain the purity of the supplied breathing air. For this reason, an air compressor in use must be located so that the air intake component is not drawing from areas that contain:

- Combustion exhaust from vehicles or the compressor itself.

- Plant process exhaust, which should be exhausted to the outside by the facility's ventilation system.

- Contaminated air from hazardous work areas.

(i)(5)(ii) Low moisture content of ambient air

The moisture content of compressed air must be kept to a minimum to prevent freezing of respirator valves at cold temperatures, which can cause blockages in the flow of breathing air. To ensure a low moisture content, the dew point at 1 atmosphere must be 10° F (5.56° C) below the ambient temperature (e.g., in plant).

Are there any systems for keeping moisture from getting into a compressor?

Water traps or desiccators can keep moisture out of a compressor. These systems remove the water from the air as it is run through the compressor, ensuring a certain level of dryness when it comes out. Such systems, like all other parts of a compressor, must be maintained in accord with the manufacturer's instructions to properly remove the moisture.

(i)(5)(iii) Inline air purification

Suitable air-purifying beds and filters must be used in the supply lines to ensure delivery of a continuous flow of Grade D breathing air to the respirator user. (A sorbent bed is a filter designed to capture impurities in the air.) You must maintain, refurbish, or replace inline sorbent beds and filters as specified by the equipment manufacturer.

(i)(5)(iv) Tracking of bed and filter changes

You must ensure that a tag is maintained at/on the compressor with a note indicating when the sorbent beds and filters were last changed. The notation must include the signature of the person you have authorized to perform the bed and filter maintenance. Only a tag indicating the most recent filter and bed changes needs to be retained at/on the compressor.

Requirements Regarding Carbon Monoxide

You must take certain precautions in regard to carbon monoxide when using compressors with atmosphere-supplying respirators.

These precautions are required because:

- Exposure to carbon monoxide above certain levels can be fatal.

- Sources of this potentially lethal gas are fairly common in many worksites. (In fact, one source of carbon monoxide is the exhaust from the compressor itself.)

- You will not be able to detect the presence of carbon monoxide because it is an odorless gas.

- The types of precautions you will need to take depend on the type of compressor you use.

(i)(6) Compressors that are not oil lubricated

With this type of compressor, you must ensure that carbon monoxide in the breathing air is less than or equal to 10 ppm. This can be achieved by:

- Locating the compressor's air intake component in an area free of contaminants

- Conducting continuous or frequent monitoring of the breathing air supply

- Using inline carbon monoxide filters

- Using high-temperature alarms or shut-off devices

(i)(7) Compressors that are oil lubricated

With this type of compressor, carbon monoxide can be generated when oil enters the combustion chamber and is partially combusted. Therefore, you must ensure that the compressor operates with a carbon monoxide alarm or a high-temperature alarm. Carbon monoxide alarms provide better protection than high-temperature alarms because the high-temperature alarms only detect carbon monoxide generated in the combustion chamber, and not carbon monoxide resulting from a poorly located compressor intake. Furthermore, high temperature alarms are installed more for the purpose of protecting the compressor from damage than for guarding employees from exposure to carbon monoxide. Because of this, the alarm component of the system is often located with the alarm sensor where it may not be heard by the respirator users. Consequently, if the compressor has only a high-temperature alarm, you must ensure that air quality is frequently monitored to confirm that carbon monoxide levels stay below 10 ppm.

How often should I check on carbon monoxide levels?

Periodic monitoring for carbon monoxide is acceptable when using newer, well-maintained compressors. Continuous monitoring, however, is recommended for older compressors. In older equipment, oil may enter the air supply more readily due to piston ring or cylinder wear. Continuous monitoring also should be conducted for rented or second-hand compressors because the maintenance history is likely to be unknown or uncertain.

How do I check carbon monoxide levels?

Carbon monoxide levels can be tested with two general types of devices:

- Direct reading instruments that use electrochemical sensors

- Chemical detector tubes

Although the electrochemical devices tend to be more expensive, they are also more accurate (i.e., they have a 5 percent error rate). Also, such devices must be calibrated periodically (usually monthly) to achieve accurate readings. Calibration services provide traceable calibrations using a wide variety of multimeter devices.

Newer generations of electrochemical sensors use a meter with built-in advanced features that enhance reliability and repeatability. These may also have auto-zero features to eliminate manual calibration. The carbon monoxide meter shows carbon monoxide levels (0–1000 ppm) on a large, backlit liquid crystal display (LCD) and have hold functions to store and display the maximum carbon monoxide level.

Chemical detector tubes have an error rate of 10 to 15 percent. Carbon monoxide filters (i.e., filters that convert carbon monoxide to carbon dioxide) with color-change indicators may not be used as carbon monoxide monitors because the color change indicates the presence of moisture, not carbon monoxide.

Other devices, such as carbon monoxide probes and aspirator kits provide additional functions. Probes have

both light-emitting diodes (LED) that provide backlighting for indicators and beepers that trigger with increasing frequency as carbon monoxide levels rise. Optional aspirator kits let the user draw flue gas samples up to 370 degrees C (700 degrees F).

Must each of these methods be used for compressors that are not oil lubricated?

No, you must use whichever of the above methods are necessary to ensure that carbon monoxide does not contaminate the breathing air. In some cases, one method may be all that is needed. In other cases, you may be required to use more than one of these methods.

You must evaluate your own worksite conditions to determine which measures are needed to prevent carbon monoxide from contaminating breathing air.

(i)(8) Precautions regarding couplings

You must ensure that couplings used on airlines for atmosphere-supplying respirators are *incompatible* with outlets for nonbreathable worksite air or other gas systems. This precaution must be taken to avoid the chance of inadvertently connecting a respirator to a source other than the breathing air. Such a mistake could result in serious illness or death. Also, you must ensure that at no time is an asphyxiating substance introduced into a respirator's airlines. For example, an inert gas such as nitrogen must not be used to purge or clean breathing airlines.

(i)(9) Labeling of breathing gas containers

You must ensure that breathing air containers are labeled in keeping with the NIOSH respirator certification standard (42 CFR 84). The NIOSH standard incorporates ANSI's Method of Marking Portable Compressed Gas Containers to Identify Material Contained (Z48.1-1971). Proper labeling of containers will avoid the possibility of confusion when connecting the breathing air source to the respirator.

CHECKLIST FOR BREATHING AIR QUALITY AND USE

√ Check that at your facility:

General

❑ Compressed breathing air meets the requirements for Grade D breathing air.

❑ Compressed oxygen is not used in respirators that have previously used compressed air.

❑ Oxygen concentrations greater than 23.5 percent are used only in equipment designed for oxygen service or distribution.

❑ Breathing air couplings are incompatible with outlets for other gas systems.

❑ Breathing gas containers are marked in accord with the NIOSH certification standard.

❑ Carbon monoxide levels are monitored for both oil and gas compressors.

Breathing Air Cylinders

❑ Cylinders are tested and maintained according to DOT 49 CFR Parts 173 and 178.

❑ A certificate of analysis for breathing air has been obtained from the supplier.

❑ Moisture content in the cylinder does not exceed a dew point of -50°F at 1 atmosphere pressure.

Compressors

❑ Are constructed and situated to prevent contaminated air from getting into the system.

❑ Are set up to minimize the moisture content.

❑ Are equipped with in-line air-purifying sorbent beds and filters that are maintained or replaced following manufacturer's instructions.

❑ Are tagged with information on the most recent change date of the filter and an authorizing signature.

❑ Carbon monoxide does not exceed 10 ppm in the breathing air from compressors that are not oil-lubricated.

❑ High-temperature or carbon monoxide alarms are used on oil-lubricated compressors; monitor the air often enough to ensure that carbon monoxide does not exceed 10 ppm if only a high-temperature alarm is used.

Section (j): Identification of filters, cartridges and canisters

This section of the standard requires you to ensure that all filters, cartridges and canisters used are labeled and color coded with the NIOSH approval label. You must also ensure that the label is not removed and remains legible.

To fulfill these requirements, you should adopt appropriate procedures for ensuring that:

- Only NIOSH-certified filters, cartridges and canisters are used
- Labels are not removed, defaced, or obscured during respirator usage

    Your written respiratory protection program must include these provisions.

What is included on the NIOSH label?

The label clearly states the class of contaminants for which the filter, cartridge, or canister may be used (e.g., permissible particulate respirator filter for dusts, fumes and mists, including asbestos-containing dusts and mists and radionuclides). The NIOSH certification number and any limitations or precautions are also included on the label.

What is the purpose of the label?

The NIOSH label serves several purposes. It ensures selection of the appropriate cartridge/canister for the contaminants found in the workplace. Also, it permits the employee using the respirator to check and confirm that the respirator has the appropriate filters before the respirator is used. Further, the color coding scheme allows fellow employees, supervisors and the respiratory protection program administrator to readily determine that the worker is using the appropriate filter.

Can I write the date of initial use on the label?

Yes, marking the initial use date on the label can be done if it does not obscure the information on the label.

Section (k): Training and information

This section of the Respiratory Protection standard requires you to train your employees on all the essential elements that help protect the employees while they use respirators. Some of these components answer the following questions, among others: why the respirator is needed; how must the respirator be maintained; and, what steps should the employee take when respirators fail to function or in emergency situations. Training on fit testing for negative pressure respirators and the need for user seal checks after donning respirators is important for the employee to determine how well a respirator fits. Employee training is a critical part of a successful respiratory protection program and is essential for correct respirator use. You must provide training to your employees who are required to wear respirators.

(k)(1) Content of training

You must ensure that each worker can demonstrate knowledge of at least the following:

- **Why the respirator is necessary and how improper fit, usage and maintenance can make the respirator ineffective.**

  - Training must include the identification of hazards, the extent of employee exposure to those hazards, and the potential health effects of exposure. The training that is required under the Hazard Communication standard (29 CFR 1910.1200) can satisfy this requirement for chemical hazards. Employees must understand that proper fit, usage, and maintenance of respirators is critical to ensure that they can perform their protective function.

- **The limitations and capabilities of the selected respirator.**

  - Training must address how the respirator operates. Included must be an explanation of how the respirator provides protection by filtering the air, absorbing the gas or vapor, or by supplying a clean source of air. Limitations on the use of the equipment, such as prohibitions against using an air-purifying respirator in an IDLH atmosphere, and why not, must also be explained.

  - Training must address the possibility of respirator malfunction and the development of emergency situations specific to the worksite. Employees must understand what procedures are to be followed in such circumstances, and which procedures require use of a different respirator.

- **How to properly select cartridges and canisters and know the assigned cartridge and canister change schedules for the devices selected.**

  - Training must address how to use the respirator effectively in terms of the use of cartridges and canisters, the exposures the cartridges are designed to address, and knowledge of the estimated service life of cartridges.

- **How to use the respirator effectively in emergency situations.**

  - Training must address how to use a respirator effectively in emergency situations, which are occurrences such as, but not limited to, respirator malfunctions or failures, rupture of containers, or failure of control equipment that may or does

result in an uncontrolled substantial release of an airborne contaminant. Respirators malfunction on occasion, work routines change, and emergency situations occur that require a different respirator. The training program must discuss these possibilities and the procedures the employer has established to deal with them. Such training is necessary when respirators are to be used in IDLH situations, including oxygen-deficient atmospheres, such as those that occur in firefighting, rescue operations and confined area entry.

- **How to inspect, put on and remove, use and check the seals of the respirator.**

  - You must train employees how to recognize problems that may decrease the effectiveness of the respirator and what steps to follow if a problem is detected, such as the person to whom problems should be reported and where replacement equipment can be obtained if needed. If specialized personnel conduct inspections, individual respirator wearers only need to be taught about the portions of the inspection process that are their responsibility. You must also cover how to properly put on and remove the respirator to ensure that respirator fit in the workplace is as close as possible to the fit obtained during fit testing. Employees must be trained to perform user seal checks. *(See Appendix B-1 of the standard.)*

- **The respirator maintenance and storage procedures.**

  - The extent of training required may vary according to workplace conditions. If employees are individually responsible for storing and maintaining respirators, detailed training may be necessary. If specialized personnel perform these functions, employees only need to be informed of the general maintenance and storage procedures.

- **How to recognize medical signs and symptoms that may limit or prevent effective use of the respirator.**

  - You must instruct employees to recognize medical signs and symptoms, such as shortness of breath or dizziness that may limit or prevent effective use of respirators.

- **The general requirements of the Respiratory Protection standard.**

  - You must ensure that employees are aware, in general, of your obligations under the standard. This discussion need not focus on the standard's provisions but could, for example, simply inform employees that employers are obligated to develop a written program, properly select respirators, evaluate respirator use, correct

deficiencies in respirator use, conduct medical evaluations, provide for the maintenance, storage and cleaning of respirators, and retain and provide access to specific records.

Do I need to follow a particular format?

No. As long as the required topics are addressed, you can use whatever training method is effective. Prepared materials, such as audiovisual and slide presentations, formal classroom instruction, informal discussions during safety meetings, training programs developed or conducted by unions or respirator manufacturers, or a combination of these methods may be used.

In what sense are employees expected to be able to "demonstrate knowledge" of proper respirator use based on the training?

You must ensure that, before an employee is required to use a respirator in the workplace, he or she understands the information provided and can use the respirator properly. This can be done by reviewing the training with the employee either orally or in writing, and by reviewing the employee's hands-on use of respirators.

(k)(2) Comprehension of training

Training must be conducted in a manner that is understandable to your employees. This means that your program should be tailored to your employees' education level and language background.

(k)(3) Timing of training

You must provide the required training prior to having an employee use a respirator in the workplace.

(k)(4) Portability of training

If you can demonstrate that a new employee has received training within the last 12 months and can demonstrate the necessary knowledge, you are not required to repeat this training. In cases where training in some elements is lacking or inadequate, you are required to provide training in those elements. Previous training that has been transported with the employee (i.e., not repeated initially) must be provided no later than 12 months from the date of the previous training.

(k)(5) Retraining

You must retrain employees in the proper use of respirators annually. You must also retrain employees when:

- Changes in the workplace or the type of respirator make previous training obsolete.

- The knowledge and skill necessary to use the respirator properly has not been retained by the employee.

- Any other situation arises in which retraining

appears necessary to ensure safe respirator use.

(k)(6) Information for voluntary respirator users

For employees who choose to wear a respirator but are not required to do so, you are required to provide the advisory information in *Appendix D* of the standard. A copy of the standard is provided in Attachment 3 of this guide. This basic information on the proper use of respirators can be presented to the employee either verbally or in written form. Training is usually not required for employees who are not required to wear respirators, i.e., for employees who are wearing respirators voluntarily.

CHECKLIST FOR TRAINING AND INFORMATION

√ Check that your facility provides the following:

Demonstration of employees' knowledge of:

❑ Why the respirator is necessary and the consequences of improper fit, use, or maintenance.

❑ The limitations and capabilities of the respirator.

❑ How to effectively use the respirator in emergency situations, including respirator malfunction.

❑ How to inspect, put on, remove, use and check the seals of the respirator.

❑ Maintenance and storage procedures.

❑ The general requirements of the Respiratory Protection standard.

❑ How to recognize medical signs and symptoms that may limit or prevent effective use of the respirator.

√ Check that your facility satisfies the general requirements of the respirator standard by providing the following:

❑ Training that is understandable to employees.

❑ Training prior to employee use of a respirator.

❑ Retraining as specified below:

- Annually.

- Upon changes in workplace conditions that affect respirator use.

- When knowledge and skills for respirator use are not retained by the employee.

- Whenever retraining appears necessary to ensure safe respirator use.

❑ *Appendix D of the standard* to voluntary users.

Section (l): Program Evaluation

(l)(1) Conducting program evaluations

You must perform evaluations of the workplace as necessary to make sure that your written respiratory protection program is working effectively.

How often do I need to evaluate my written respiratory protection program?

You do not need to review your respiratory protection program according to any fixed schedule. The frequency with which you need to evaluate your respiratory protection program will depend on the complexity and/or variability of the program and factors such as:

- The type and extent of hazards in your workplace.

- The types of respirators used by your employees.

- The number of your employees who use respirators.

- The amount of experience your respirator-wearing employeess have in using respirators.

You must evaluate respirator use with sufficient frequency to ensure that all elements of the respiratory protection program are being effectively implemented.

(l)(2) Consulting with employees

You must regularly consult with employees required to wear respirators to assess their views on the effectiveness of the respiratory protection program and to identify any problems that they may be encountering with the use of respirators. You must correct any problems that are identified.

At a minimum, you must assess:

- Whether proper fit of respirators is being achieved, and whether respirator use is interfering with effective work performance.

- Whether appropriate respirators have been selected.

- Whether respirators are being properly used.

- Whether respirators are being properly maintained.

When I consult with my employees, what should I ask them?

You may want to ask your workers questions such as:

- Does your respirator interfere with your hearing or vision?

- Do you experience fatigue or have difficulty breathing during respirator use?

- Does your respirator restrict your movements or interfere with your job performance in any way?

- Is your respirator uncomfortable?

- Are you confident that you are using your respirator correctly?
- Are you confident that your respirator is performing adequately?

CHECKLIST FOR PROGRAM EVALUATION

√ Check that your facility:

❑ Conducts workplace evaluations as necessary to ensure that the written respiratory protection program is being effectively implemented.

❑ Regularly consults with employees required to wear respirators to assess their views on the respiratory protection program and to identify problems with respirator fit, selection, use and maintenance.

❑ Corrects any problems identified during assessments.

Section (m): Recordkeeping

You must retain certain records to:

- assist you in auditing the adequacy of your respiratory protection program

- facilitate employee involvement

- allow OSHA to inspect your records and make compliance determinations

(m)(1) Medical evaluation records

Records of medical evaluations required by *paragraph (e)* of the standard must be retained and made available to the employees in accord with OSHA's Access to Employee Exposure and Medical Records standard (29 CFR 1910.1020).

(m)(2) Respirator fit testing records

You are required to retain written records of the qualitative and quantitative fit tests administered to your employees. These records need to include:

- The name or identification of the worker tested.

- The type of fit test performed.

- The make, model and size of the respirator tested.

- The date of the fit test.

- Pass/fail results if a qualitative fit test (QLFT) is used, or the fit factor and strip chart recording or other record of the test results if a quantitative fit test (QNFT) is used.

How long do I need to retain fit test records?

Fit test records must be retained for respirator users until the next fit test is administered.

Do I need to retain records of fit tests for employees who are no longer using respirators?

No, fit test records do not need to be retained for these employees.

(m)(3) Written respiratory protection program

You must retain a written copy of your current respiratory protection program.

(m)(4) Access to records

Written materials required to be retained must be made available upon request to the affected employees, their designated representatives (29 CFR 1910.1020), and to OSHA. (See also 29 CFR 1910.1020 at: http://www.osha.gov/pls/oshaweb/owadisp.show_document?p_table=STANDARDS&p_id=10027.)

Do I need to allow employees and OSHA to make copies of these materials?

Yes, you need to make these materials available for inspection and for copying.

Must employees be allowed access to the records of other employees?

No, each affected employe can have access to his or her records only.

CHECKLIST FOR RECORDKEEPING

√ Check that your facility does the following:

❑ Retains records of medical evaluations.

❑ Retains fit testing records.

❑ Retains a copy of the current respiratory protection program.

❑ Provides access to the above records by affected employees and OSHA.

Attachment 1:
APF Glossary and definitions

The preamble to the final rule for Assigned Protection Factors (APF) includes a glossary (see 71 FR 50122; August 24, 2006) that provides an auxiliary list of terms used in the APF rulemaking and throughout the preamble to the APF final rule. In the glossary portion, there is both a list of acronyms used in the APF rule and a list of definitions, in addition to the definitions in the APF rulemaking for Assigned Protection Factor and Maximum Use Concentration (MUC). The glossary contains acronyms and terms from the final Respiratory Protection standard (29 CFR 1910.134) each of which is printed in brown italics and is highlighted with an asterisk (*). The purpose of this glossary in this Small Entity Compliance Guide, is to provide those same acronyms and terms from the final Respiratory Protection standard, and to provide the new definitions for APFs and MUCs from the APF rulemaking in one place for ease of review. A copy of the Respiratory Protection standard is provided in Attachment 3. *(See 71 FR 50122, August 24, 2006, for a copy of the APF standard.)*

This glossary specifies the terms represented by acronyms and provides definitions of other terms used frequently in the preamble to the final rule. This glossary does not change the legal requirements in this final rule, nor is it intended to impose new regulatory requirements on the regulated community.

Acronyms

ACGIH	American Conference of Governmental Industrial Hygienists
AIHA	American Industrial Hygiene Association
ANSI	American National Standards Institute
APF	Assigned Protection Factor (see definition)
APR	Air-purifying respirator (see definition)
Ci	Concentration measured inside the respirator facepiece
Co	Concentration measured outside the respirator
DFM	Dust, fume, and mist filter
DOP	Dioctylphthalate (see definition)
EPF	Effective Protection Factor (see definition below under "Protection factor study")
HEPA	High efficiency particulate air filter (see definition)
IDLH	Immediately dangerous to life or health (see definition)
LANL	Los Alamos National Laboratory
LASL	Los Alamos Scientific Laboratory
LLNL	Lawrence Livermore National Laboratory
MSHA	Mine Safety and Health Administration
MUC	Maximum Use Concentration (see definition)
NFPA	National Fire Protection Association
NIOSH	National Institute for Occupational Safety and Health
NRC	Nuclear Regulatory Commission
OSHA	Occupational Safety and Health Administration
OSH Act	The Occupational Safety and Health Act of 1970 (29 U.S.C. 655, 657, 665).
PAPR	Powered air-purifying respirator (see definition)
PEL	Permissible Exposure Limit (see definition)
PPF	Program Protection Factor (see definition below under "Protection factor study")
QLFT	Qualitative fit test (see definition)
QNFT	Quantitative fit test (see definition)
RDL	Respirator Decision Logic (see definition)
REL	Recommended Exposure Limit (see definition)
SAR	Supplied-air (or airline) respirator (see definition)
SCBA	Self-contained breathing apparatus (see definition)
SWPF	Simulated Workplace Protection Factor (see definition below under "Protection factor study")
TLV	Threshold Limit Value (see definition)
WPF	Workplace Protection Factor (see definition below under "Protection factor study")

Definitions

Terms preceded by an asterisk (*) refer to definitions that can be found in paragraph (b) ("Definitions") of OSHA's Respiratory Protection standard (29 CFR 1910.134).

Air-purifying respirator: A respirator with an air-purifying filter, cartridge, or canister that removes specific air contaminants by passing ambient air through the air-purifying element.

Assigned protection factor (APF): means the workplace level of respiratory protection that a respirator or class of respirators is expected to provide to employees when the employer implements a continuing, effective respiratory protection program as specified by this section.

*Atmosphere-supplying respirator: A respirator that supplies the respirator user with breathing air from a source independent of the ambient atmosphere, and includes SARs and SCBA units.

*Canister or cartridge: A container with a filter, sorbent, or catalyst, or combination of these items, which removes specific contaminants from the air passed through the container.

Continuous flow respirator: An atmosphere-supplying respirator that provides a continuous flow of breathable air to the respirator facepiece.

*Demand respirator: An atmosphere-supplying respirator that admits breathing air to the facepiece only when a negative pressure is created inside the facepiece by inhalation.

Dioctylphthalate (DOP): An aerosolized agent used for quantitative fit testing.

Elastomeric: A respirator facepiece made of a natural or synthetic elastic material such as natural rubber, silicone, or synthetic rubber.

*Emergency situation: Any occurrence such as, but not limited to, equipment failure, rupture of containers, or failure of control equipment that may or does result in an uncontrolled significant release of an airborne contaminant.

*Employee exposure: Exposure to a concentration of an airborne contaminant that would occur if the employee were not using respiratory protection.

*End-of-service-life indicator (ESLI): A system that warns the respirator user of the approach of the end of adequate respiratory protection, for example, that the sorbent is approaching saturation or is no longer effective.

*Escape-only respirator: A respirator intended to be used only for emergency exit.

*Filter or air-purifying element: A component used in respirators to remove solid or liquid aerosols from the inspired air.

*Filtering facepiece (or dust mask): A negative pressure particulate respirator with a filter as an integral part of the facepiece or with the entire facepiece composed of the filtering medium.

*Fit factor: A quantitative estimate of the fit of a particular respirator to a specific individual, and typically estimates the ratio of the concentration of a substance in ambient air to its concentration inside the respirator when worn.

*Fit test: The use of a protocol to qualitatively or quantitatively evaluate the fit of a respirator on an individual.

*Helmet: A rigid respiratory inlet covering that also provides head protection against impact and penetration.

*High-efficiency particulate air filter (HEPA): A filter that is at least 99.97% efficient in removing monodispersed particles of 0.3 micrometers in diameter. The equivalent NIOSH 42 CFR 84 particulate filters are the N100, R100, and P100 filters.

*Hood: A respiratory inlet covering that completely covers the head and neck and may also cover portions of the shoulders and torso.

*Immediately dangerous to life or health (IDLH): An atmosphere that poses an immediate threat to life, would cause irreversible adverse health effects, or would impair an individual's ability to escape from a dangerous atmosphere.

*Interior structural firefighting: The physical activity of fire suppression, rescue or both, inside of buildings or enclosed structures which are involved in a fire situation beyond the incipient stage. (See 29 CFR 1910.155).

*Loose-fitting facepiece: A respiratory inlet covering that is designed to form a partial seal with the face.

*Maximum use concentration (MUC): The maximum atmospheric concentration of a hazardous substance from which an employee can be expected to be protected when wearing a respirator, and is determined by the assigned protection factor of the respirator or class of respirators and the exposure limit of the hazardous substance. The MUC can be determined mathematically by multiplying the assigned protection factor specified for a respirator by the required OSHA permissible exposure limit, short-term exposure limit, or ceiling limit. When no OSHA exposure limit is available for a hazardous substance, an employer must determine an MUC on the basis of relevant available information and informed professional judgment.

*Negative pressure respirator (tight-fitting): A respirator in which the air pressure inside the facepiece is negative during inhalation with respect to the ambient air pressure outside the respirator.

*Oxygen deficient atmosphere: An atmosphere with an oxygen content below 19.5% by volume.

Permissible Exposure Limit (PEL): An occupational exposure limit specified by OSHA.

*Physician or other licensed healthcare professional (PLHCP): An individual whose legally permitted scope of practice (i.e., license, registration, or certification) allows him or her to independently provide, or be delegated the responsibility to provide, some or all of the healthcare services required by paragraph (e) of this section.

*Positive pressure respirator: A respirator in which the pressure inside the respiratory inlet covering exceeds the ambient air pressure outside the respirator.

Powered air-purifying respirator (PAPR): An air-purifying respirator that uses a blower to force the ambient air through air-purifying elements to the inlet covering.

Pressure demand respirator: A positive pressure atmosphere-supplying respirator that admits breathing air to the facepiece when the positive pressure is reduced inside the facepiece by inhalation.

Protection factor study: A study that determines the protection provided by a respirator during use. This determination generally is accomplished by measuring the ratio of the concentration of an airborne contaminant (e.g., hazardous substance) outside the respirator (C_o) to the concentration inside the respirator (C_i) (i.e., C_o/C_i). Therefore, as the ratio between C_o and C_i increases, the protection factor increases, indicating an increase in the level of protection provided to employees by the respirator. Four types of protection factor studies are:

Effective Protection Factor (EPF) study - a study, conducted in the workplace, that measures the protection provided by a properly selected, fit-tested, and functioning respirator when used intermittently for only some fraction of the total workplace exposure time (i.e., sampling is conducted during periods when respirators are worn and not worn). EPFs are not directly comparable to Workplace Protection Factor (WPF) values because the determinations include both the time spent in contaminated atmospheres with and without respiratory protection; therefore, EPFs usually underestimate the protection afforded by a respirator that is used continuously in the workplace.

Program Protection Factor (PPF) study - a study that estimates the protection provided by a respirator within a specific respirator program. Like the EPF, it is focused not only on the respirator's performance, but also the effectiveness of the complete respirator program. PPFs are affected by all factors of the program, including respirator selection and maintenance, user training and motivation, work activities and program administration.

Workplace Protection Factor (WPF) study - a study, conducted under actual conditions of use in the workplace, that measures the protection provided by a properly selected, fit-tested, and functioning respirator, when the respirator is worn correctly and used as part of a comprehensive respirator program that is in compliance with OSHA's Respiratory Protection standard at 29 CFR 1910.134. Measurements of C_o and C_i are obtained only while the respirator is being worn during performance of normal work tasks (i.e., samples are not collected when the respirator is not being worn). As the degree of protection afforded by the respirator increases, the WPF increases.

Simulated Workplace Protection Factor (SWPF) study - a study, conducted in a controlled laboratory setting and in which C_o and C_i sampling is performed while the respirator user performs a series of set exercises. The laboratory setting is used to control many of the variables found in workplace studies, while the exercises simulate the work activities of respirator users. This type of study is designed to determine the optimum performance of respirators by reducing the impact of sources of variability through maintenance of tightly controlled study conditions.

Qualitative fit test (QLFT): A pass/fail fit test to assess the adequacy of respirator fit that relies on the individual's response to the test agent.

Quantitative fit test (QNFT): An assessment of the adequacy of respirator fit by numerically measuring the amount of leakage into the respirator.

Recommended Exposure Limit (REL): An occupational exposure level recommended by NIOSH.

Respirator Decision Logic (RDL): Respirator selection guidance developed by NIOSH that contains a set of respirator protection factors.

Respiratory inlet covering: That portion of a respirator that forms the protective barrier between the user's respiratory tract and an air-purifying device or breathing air source, or both. It may be a facepiece, helmet, hood, suit, or a mouthpiece respirator with nose clamp.

Self-contained breathing apparatus (SCBA): An atmosphere-supplying respirator for which the breathing air source is designed to be carried by the user.

Supplied-air respirator (or airline) respirator (SAR): An atmosphere-supplying respirator for which the source of breathing air is not designed to be carried by the user.

Threshold Limit Value (TLV): An occupational exposure level recommended by ACGIH.

Tight-fitting facepiece: A respiratory inlet covering that forms a complete seal with the face.

User seal check: An action conducted by the respirator user to determine if the respirator is properly seated to the face.

OSHA
Occupational Safety and
Health Administration

Attachment 2:
Checklists

CHECKLIST FOR PERMISSIBLE PRACTICE

√ Check all that apply:

Hazard Determination

Is there a hazardous atmosphere in your workplace, which has (check all that apply):

❑ Insufficient oxygen

❑ Harmful levels of chemical, biological, or radiological contaminants

❑ Known and reasonably foreseeable emergencies related to...

❑ Unknown exposure levels or exposures to substances without an OSHA PEL

If you did not check any of the boxes above, the Respiratory Protection standard **does not** apply to your workplace.

If you checked any of the boxes above, the Respiratory Protection standard **may** apply to your workplace.

OSHA requires use of the following methods to control the hazardous atmosphere(s) in your workplace:

❑ Engineering controls, such as ventilation, isolation or enclosure of the work process, or substitution of non-hazardous materials for the materials that pose respiratory hazards; and

❑ Administrative controls, such as worker rotation, or scheduling major maintenance for weekends or times when few workers are present.

When engineering controls are not feasible, or while engineering controls are being installed or maintained, or whenever there is an emergency, appropriate respirators **must** be used.

Does your workplace have (check the box to indicate yes, and check all that apply):

❑ Sufficient engineering controls to prevent illness or diseases caused by breathing hazardous air in the workplace

❑ Sufficient administrative controls to prevent illness

If you did not check **both** of the boxes above, the Respiratory Protection standard **does apply** to your workplace, and you must develop a written respiratory protection program that is specific to your workplace.

CHECKLIST FOR RESPIRATORY PROTECTION PROGRAMS

√ Does your program contain written procedures for (check all that apply):

❑ Your specific workplace

❑ Selecting respirators

❑ Medical evaluations of employees required to wear respirators

❑ Fit testing

❑ Routine and emergency respirator use

❑ Schedules for cleaning, disinfecting, storing, inspecting, repairing, discarding, and maintaining respirators

❑ Ensuring adequate air quality for supplied-air respirators

❑ Training in respiratory hazards

❑ Training in proper use and maintenance of respirators

❑ Program evaluation

❑ Ensuring that employees who voluntarily wear respirators (excluding filtering facepieces) comply with the medical evaluation and cleaning, storing and maintenance requirements of the standard

❑ A designated program administrator who is qualified to administer the program

❑ Updating the written program as necessary to account for changes in the workplace affecting respirator use

❑ Providing equipment, training and medical evaluations at no cost to employees

If you did not check all of the boxes above, your respiratory protection program **does not** meet OSHA standards.

CHECKLIST FOR RESPIRATOR SELECTION

√ Check that the following has been done at your facility:

❏ Respiratory hazards in your workplace have been identified and evaluated.

❏ Employee exposures that have not been, or cannot be, evaluated must be considered IDLH.

❏ Respirators are NIOSH-certified, and used under the conditions of certification.

❏ Respirators are selected based on the workplace hazards evaluated and workplace and user factors affecting respirator performance and reliability.

❏ Respirators are selected based on the APFs and calculated MUCs.

❏ A sufficient number of respirator sizes and models are provided for selection purposes.

For IDLH atmospheres:

❏ Full facepiece pressure demand SARs with auxiliary SCBA unit or full facepiece pressure demand SCBAs, with a minimum service life of 30 minutes, are provided.

❏ Respirators used for escape only are NIOSH-certified for the atmosphere in which they will be used.

❏ Oxygen deficient atmospheres must be considered IDLH (d)(2)(B)(iii).

For Non-IDLH atmospheres:

❏ Respirators selected are appropriate for the APFs and MUCs.

❏ Respirators selected are appropriate for the chemical nature and physical form of the contaminant.

❏ Air-purifying respirators used for protection against gases and vapors are equipped with ESLIs or a change schedule has been implemented.

❏ Air-purifying respirators used for protection against particulates are equipped with NIOSH-certified HEPA filters or other filters certified by NIOSH for particulates under 42 CFR part 84.

CHECKLIST FOR MEDICAL EVALUATION

√ Check that the following has been done at your facility:

❏ All employees have been evaluated to determine their ability to wear a respirator prior to being fit tested for or wearing a respirator for the first time in your workplace.

❏ A physician or other licensed healthcare professional (PLHCP) has been identified to perform the medical evaluations.

❏ The medical evaluations obtain the information requested in *Sections 1 and 2, Part A of Appendix C of the standard, 29 CFR 1910.134. (See Attachment 3)*

❏ Employees are provided follow-up medical exams if they answer positively to any of *questions 1 through 8 in Section 2, Part A of Appendix C* of the standard, or if their medical examination reveals that a follow-up exam is needed.

❏ Medical evaluations are administered confidentially during normal work hours, and in a manner that is understandable to employees.

❏ Employees are provided the opportunity to discuss the medical evaluation results with the PLHCP.

❏ The following supplemental information is provided to the PLHCP before he or she makes a decision about respirator use:
  • Type and weight of the respirator.
  • Duration and frequency of respirator use.
  • Expected physical work effort.
  • Additional protective clothing to be worn.
  • Potential temperature and humidity extremes.
  • Written copies of the respiratory protection program and the Respiratory Protection standard are provided to the PLHCP.

❏ Written recommendations are obtained from the PLHCP regarding each employee's ability to wear a respirator, and that the PLHCP has given the worker a copy of these recommendations.

❏ Employees who are medically unable to wear a negative pressure respirator are provided with a powered air-purifying respirator (PAPR) if they are found by the PLHCP to be medically able to use a PAPR. *(29 CFR 1910.1034(e)(6)(ii).)*

Employees are given additional medical evaluations when:

❏ The employee reports symptoms related to his or her ability to use a respirator.

❏ The PLHCP, respiratory protection program administrator, or supervisor determines that a medical reevaluation is necessary.

❏ Information from the respiratory protection program suggests a need for reevaluation.

❏ Workplace conditions have changed in a way that could potentially place an increased physiological burden on the employee.

CHECKLIST FOR FIT TESTING

√ Check all the fit tests listed below that are used at your facility:

❑ Employees who are using tight-fitting respirator facepieces have passed an appropriate fit test prior to being required to use a respirator.

❑ Fit testing is conducted with the same make, model, style and size that the employee will be expected to use at the worksite.

❑ Fit tests are conducted annually and when different respirator facepieces are to be used.

❑ Provisions are made to conduct additional fit tests in the event of physical changes in the employee that may affect respirator fit.

❑ Employees are given the opportunity to select a different respirator facepiece, and be retested if their respirator fit is unacceptable to them.

❑ Fit tests are administered using OSHA-accepted QNFT or QLFT protocols.

❑ QLFT is only used to fit test either PAPRs, SCBAs, or negative pressure APRs that must achieve a fit factor of 100 or less.

❑ QNFT is used in all situations where a negative pressure respirator is intended to protect workers from contaminant concentrations greater than 10 times the PEL.

❑ When QNFT is used to fit negative pressure respirators, a minimum fit factor of 100 is achieved for tight-fitting half facepieces and 500 for full facepieces.

For tight-fitting atmosphere-supplying respirators and powered air-purifying respirators:

❑ Fit tests are conducted in the negative pressure mode.

❑ QLFT is achieved by temporarily converting the facepiece into a negative pressure respirator with appropriate filters, or by using an identical negative pressure APR.

❑ QNFT is achieved by modifying the facepiece to allow for sampling inside the mask midway between the nose and mouth. If the facepiece is permanently converted during fit testing, the respirator is no longer approved for workplace use.

CHECKLIST FOR PROPER USE OF RESPIRATORS

√ Check your facility to be certain that:

❑ Employees using tight-fitting respirators have no conditions, such as facial hair, that would interfere with a face-to-facepiece seal or valve function.

❑ Employees wear corrective glasses, goggles, or other protective equipment in a manner that does not interfere with the face-to-facepiece seal or valve function.

❑ Employees perform user seal checks prior to each use of a tight-fitting respirator.

❑ There are procedures for conducting ongoing surveillance of the work area for conditions that affect respirator effectiveness, and that, when such conditions exist, you take steps to address those situations.

❑ Employees are permitted to leave their work area to conduct respirator maintenance, such as washing the facepiece, or to replace respirator parts.

❑ Employees do not return to their work area until their respirator has been repaired or replaced in the event of a breakthrough, a leak in the facepiece, or a change in breathing resistance.

❑ There are procedures for respirator use in IDLH atmospheres and during interior structural firefighting to ensure that: the appropriate number of standby personnel are deployed; standby personnel and workers in the IDLH environment maintain communication; standby personnel are properly trained, equipped, and prepared; you will be notified when standby personnel enter an IDLH atmosphere; and you will respond appropriately to this notification.

❑ Standby personnel are equipped with a pressure demand or other positive pressure SCBA, or a positive pressure supplied-air respirator with an escape SCBA, and appropriate retrieval equipment or other means for rescue.

❑ Procedures for interior structural firefighting require that: at least two employees enter the IDLH atmosphere and remain in contact with one another at all times; at least two standby personnel are used; and all firefighting employees use SCBAs.

CHECKLIST FOR RESPIRATOR MAINTENANCE AND CARE

√ Check to make sure that your facility has met the following requirements:

Cleaning and disinfecting:

❑ Respirators are provided that are clean, sanitary, and in good working order.

❑ Respirators are cleaned and disinfected using the procedures specified in *Appendix B-2 of the standard*.

Respirators are cleaned and disinfected:

❑ As often as necessary when issued for the exclusive use of one employee.

❑ Before being worn by different individuals.

❑ After each use for emergency use respirators.

❑ After each use for respirators used for fit testing and training.

Storage:

❑ Respirators are stored to protect them from damage from the elements, and from becoming deformed.

Emergency respirators are stored:

❑ To be accessible to the work area.

❑ In compartments marked as such.

❑ In accord with manufacturer's instructions.

Inspections:

❑ Routine-use respirators are inspected before each use and during cleaning.

❑ SCBAs and emergency respirators are inspected monthly and checked for proper functioning before and after each use.

❑ Emergency escape-only respirators are inspected before being carried into the workplace for use.

Inspections include:

❑ Check of respirator function.

❑ Tightness of connections.

❑ Condition of the facepiece, head straps, valves, cartridges, and other parts.

❑ Condition of elastomeric parts.

For SCBAs, inspections include:

❑ Check that cylinders are fully charged.

❑ Check that regulators function properly.

❑ Check that warning devices function properly.

For emergency use respirators, inspections include:

❑ Certification by documenting the inspection, and by tagging the information either to the respirator or its compartment, or storing it with inspection reports.

Repairs:

❑ Respirators that have failed inspection are taken out of service.

❑ Repairs are made only by trained personnel.

❑ Only NIOSH-certified parts are used.

❑ Reducing and admission valves, regulators and alarms are adjusted or repaired only by the manufacturer or a technician trained by the manufacturer.

CHECKLIST FOR BREATHING AIR QUALITY AND USE

√ Check that at your facility:

General

❏ Compressed breathing air meets the requirements for Grade D breathing air.

❏ Compressed oxygen is not used in respirators that have previously used compressed air.

❏ Oxygen concentrations greater than 23.5 percent are used only in equipment designed for oxygen service or distribution.

❏ Breathing air couplings are incompatible with outlets for other gas systems.

❏ Breathing gas containers are marked in accord with the NIOSH certification standard.

❏ Carbon monoxide levels are monitored for both oil and gas compressors.

Breathing Air Cylinders

❏ Cylinders are tested and maintained according to DOT 49 CFR Parts 173 and 178.

❏ A certificate of analysis for breathing air has been obtained from the supplier.

❏ Moisture content in the cylinder does not exceed a dew point of -50°F at 1 atmosphere pressure.

Compressors

❏ Are constructed and situated to prevent contaminated air from getting into the system.

❏ Are set up to minimize the moisture content.

❏ Are equipped with in-line air-purifying sorbent beds and filters that are maintained or replaced following manufacturer's instructions.

❏ Are tagged with information on the most recent change date of the filter and an authorizing signature.

❏ Carbon monoxide does not exceed 10 ppm in the breathing air from compressors that are not oil-lubricated.

❏ High-temperature or carbon monoxide alarms are used on oil-lubricated compressors; monitor the air often enough to ensure that carbon monoxide does not exceed 10 ppm if only a high-temperature alarm is used.

CHECKLIST FOR TRAINING AND INFORMATION

√ Check that your facility provides the following:

Demonstration of employees' knowledge of:

❏ Why the respirator is necessary and the consequences of improper fit, use, or maintenance.

❏ The limitations and capabilities of the respirator.

❏ How to effectively use the respirator in emergency situations, including respirator malfunction.

❏ How to inspect, put on, remove, use and check the seals of the respirator.

❏ Maintenance and storage procedures.

❏ The general requirements of the Respiratory Protection standard.

❏ How to recognize medical signs and symptoms that may limit or prevent effective use of the respirator.

√ Check that your facility satisfies the general requirements of the respirator standard by providing the following:

❏ Training that is understandable to employees.

❏ Training prior to employee use of a respirator.

❏ Retraining as specified below:

  • Annually.

  • Upon changes in workplace conditions that affect respirator use.

  • When knowledge and skills for respirator use are not retained by the employee.

  • Whenever retraining appears necessary to ensure safe respirator use.

❏ *Appendix D of the standard* to voluntary users.

CHECKLIST FOR PROGRAM EVALUATION

√ Check that your facility:

❑ Conducts workplace evaluations as necessary to ensure that the written respiratory protection program is being effectively implemented.

❑ Regularly consults with employees required to wear respirators to assess their views on the respiratory protection program and to identify problems with respirator fit, selection, use and maintenance.

❑ Corrects any problems identified during assessments.

CHECKLIST FOR RECORDKEEPING

√ Check that your facility does the following:

❑ Retains records of medical evaluations.

❑ Retains fit testing records.

❑ Retains a copy of the current respiratory protection program.

❑ Provides access to the above records by affected employees and OSHA.

OSHA®
Occupational Safety and
Health Administration

Attachment 3
Respiratory Protection Standard

This section applies to General Industry (part 1910), Shipyards (part 1915), Marine Terminals (part 1917), Longshoring (part 1918), and Construction (part 1926).

1910.134(a)
Permissible practice.

1910.134(a)(1)
In the control of those occupational diseases caused by breathing air contaminated with harmful dusts, fogs, fumes, mists, gases, smokes, sprays, or vapors, the primary objective shall be to prevent atmospheric contamination. This shall be accomplished as far as feasible by accepted engineering control measures (for example, enclosure or confinement of the operation, general and local ventilation, and substitution of less toxic materials). When effective engineering controls are not feasible, or while they are being instituted, appropriate respirators shall be used pursuant to this section.

1910.134(a)(2)
Respirators shall be provided by the employer when such equipment is necessary to protect the health of the employee. The employer shall provide the respirators which are applicable and suitable for the purpose intended. The employer shall be responsible for the establishment and maintenance of a respiratory protection program which shall include the requirements outlined in paragraph (c) of this section.

1910.134(b)
Definitions.
The following definitions are important terms used in the respiratory protection standard in this section.

Air-purifying respirator means a respirator with an air-purifying filter, cartridge, or canister that removes specific air contaminants by passing ambient air through the air-purifying element.

Assigned protection factor (APF) means the workplace level of respiratory protection that a respirator or class of respirators is expected to provide to employees when the employer implements a continuing, effective respiratory protection program as specified by this section.

Atmosphere-supplying respirator means a respirator that supplies the respirator user with breathing air from a source independent of the ambient atmosphere, and includes supplied-air respirators (SARs) and self-contained breathing apparatus (SCBA) units.

Canister or cartridge means a container with a filter, sorbent, or catalyst, or combination of these items, which removes specific contaminants from the air passed through the container.

Demand respirator means an atmosphere-supplying respirator that admits breathing air to the facepiece only when a negative pressure is created inside the facepiece by inhalation.

Emergency situation means any occurrence such as, but not limited to, equipment failure, rupture of containers, or failure of control equipment that may or does result in an uncontrolled significant release of an airborne contaminant.

Employee exposure means exposure to a concentration of an airborne contaminant that would occur if the employee were not using respiratory protection.

End-of-service-life indicator (ESLI) means a system that warns the respirator user of the approach of the end of adequate respiratory protection, for example, that the sorbent is approaching saturation or is no longer effective.

Escape-only respirator means a respirator intended to be used only for emergency exit.

Filter or air purifying element means a component used in respirators to remove solid or liquid aerosols from the inspired air.

Filtering facepiece (dust mask) means a negative pressure particulate respirator with a filter as an integral part of the facepiece or with the entire facepiece composed of the filtering medium.

Fit factor means a quantitative estimate of the fit of a particular respirator to a specific individual, and typically estimates the ratio of the concentration of a substance in ambient air to its concentration inside the respirator when worn.

Fit test means the use of a protocol to qualitatively or quantitatively evaluate the fit of a respirator on an individual. (See also Qualitative fit test QLFT and Quantitative fit test QNFT.)

Helmet means a rigid respiratory inlet covering that also provides head protection against impact and penetration.

High efficiency particulate air (HEPA) filter means a filter that is at least 99.97% efficient in removing monodisperse particles of 0.3 micrometers in diameter. The equivalent NIOSH 42 CFR 84 particulate filters are the N100, R100, and P100 filters.

Hood means a respiratory inlet covering that completely covers the head and neck and may also cover portions of the shoulders and torso.

Immediately dangerous to life or health (IDLH) means an atmosphere that poses an immediate threat to life, would cause irreversible adverse health effects, or would impair an individual's ability to escape from a dangerous atmosphere.

Interior structural firefighting means the physical activity of fire suppression, rescue or both, inside of buildings or enclosed structures which are involved in a fire situation beyond the incipient stage. (See 29 CFR 1910.155)

Loose-fitting facepiece means a respiratory inlet covering that is designed to form a partial seal with the face.

Maximum use concentration (MUC) means the maximum atmospheric concentration of a hazardous substance from which an employee can be expected to be protected when wearing a respirator, and is determined by the assigned protection factor of the respirator or class of respirators and the exposure limit of the hazardous substance. The MUC can be determined mathematically by multiplying the assigned protection factor specified for a respirator by the required OSHA permissible exposure limit, short-term exposure limit, or ceiling limit. When no OSHA exposure limit is available for a hazardous substance, an employer must determine an MUC on the basis of relevant available information and informed professional judgment.

Negative pressure respirator (tight fitting) means a respirator in which the air pressure inside the facepiece is negative during inhalation with respect to the ambient air pressure outside the respirator.

Oxygen deficient atmosphere means an atmosphere with an oxygen content below 19.5% by volume.

Physician or other licensed healthcare professional (PLHCP) means an individual whose legally permitted scope of practice (i.e., license, registration, or certification) allows him or her to independently provide, or be delegated the responsibility to provide, some or all of the healthcare services required by paragraph (e) of this section.

Positive pressure respirator means a respirator in which the pressure inside the respiratory inlet covering exceeds the ambient air pressure outside the respirator.

Powered air-purifying respirator (PAPR) means an air-purifying respirator that uses a blower to force the ambient air through air-purifying elements to the inlet covering.

Pressure demand respirator means a positive pressure atmosphere-supplying respirator that admits breathing air to the facepiece when the positive pressure is reduced inside the facepiece by inhalation.

Qualitative fit test (QLFT) means a pass/fail fit test to assess the adequacy of respirator fit that relies on the individual's response to the test agent.

Quantitative fit test (QNFT) means an assessment of the adequacy of respirator fit by numerically measuring the amount of leakage into the respirator.

Respiratory inlet covering means that portion of a respirator that forms the protective barrier between the user's respiratory tract and an air-purifying device or breathing air source, or both. It may be a facepiece, helmet, hood, suit, or a mouthpiece respirator with nose clamp.

Self-contained breathing apparatus (SCBA) means an atmosphere-supplying respirator for which the breathing air source is designed to be carried by the user.

Service life means the period of time that a respirator, filter or sorbent, or other respiratory equipment provides adequate protection to the wearer.

Supplied-air respirator (SAR) or airline respirator means an atmosphere-supplying respirator for which the source of breathing air is not designed to be carried by the user.

This section means this Respiratory Protection standard.

Tight-fitting facepiece means a respiratory inlet covering that forms a complete seal with the face.

User seal check means an action conducted by the respirator user to determine if the respirator is properly seated to the face.

1910.134(c)
Respiratory protection program.
This paragraph requires the employer to develop and implement a written respiratory protection program with required worksite-specific procedures and elements for required respirator use. The program must be administered by a suitably trained program administrator. In addition, certain program elements may be required for voluntary use to prevent potential hazards associated with the use of the respirator.

> Note: The *Small Entity Compliance Guide* contains criteria for the selection of a program administrator and a sample program that meets the requirements of this paragraph.

1910.134(c)(1)
In any workplace where respirators are necessary to protect the health of the employee or whenever respirators are required by the employer, the employer shall establish and implement a written respiratory protection program with worksite-specific procedures. The program shall be updated as necessary to reflect those changes in workplace conditions that affect respirator use. The employer shall include in the program the following provisions of this section, as applicable:

1910.134(c)(1)(i)
Procedures for selecting respirators for use in the workplace;

1910.134(c)(1)(ii)
Medical evaluations of employees required to use respirators;

1910.134(c)(1)(iii)
Fit testing procedures for tight-fitting respirators;

1910.134(c)(1)(iv)
Procedures for proper use of respirators in routine and reasonably foreseeable emergency situations;

1910.134(c)(1)(v)
Procedures and schedules for cleaning, disinfecting, storing, inspecting, repairing, discarding, and otherwise maintaining respirators;

1910.134(c)(1)(vi)
Procedures to ensure adequate air quality, quantity, and flow of breathing air for atmosphere-supplying respirators;

1910.134(c)(1)(vii)
Training of employees in the respiratory hazards to which they are potentially exposed during routine and emergency situations;

1910.134(c)(1)(viii)
Training of employees in the proper use of respirators, including putting on and removing them, any limitations on their use, and their maintenance; and

1910.134(c)(1)(ix)
Procedures for regularly evaluating the effectiveness of the program.

1910.134(c)(2)
Where respirator use is not required:

1910.134(c)(2)(i)
An employer may provide respirators at the request of employees or permit employees to use their own respirators, if the employer determines that such respirator use will not in itself create a hazard. If the employer determines that any voluntary respirator use is permissible, the employer shall provide the respirator users with the information contained in Appendix D to this section ("Information for Employees Using Respirators When Not Required Under the Standard"); and

1910.134(c)(2)(ii)
In addition, the employer must establish and implement those elements of a written respiratory protection program necessary to ensure that any employee using a respirator voluntarily is medically able to use that respirator, and that the respirator is cleaned, stored, and maintained so that its use does not present a health hazard to the user. Exception: Employers are not required to include in a written respiratory protection program those employees whose only use of respirators involves the voluntary use of filtering facepieces (dust masks).

1910.134(c)(3)
The employer shall designate a program administrator who is qualified by appropriate training or experience that is commensurate with the complexity of the program to administer or oversee the respiratory protection program and conduct the required evaluations of program effectiveness.

1910.134(c)(4)
The employer shall provide respirators, training, and medical evaluations at no cost to the employee.

1910.134(d)

Selection of respirators.

This paragraph requires the employer to evaluate respiratory hazard(s) in the workplace, identify relevant workplace and user factors, and base respirator selection on these factors. The paragraph also specifies appropriately protective respirators for use in IDLH atmospheres, and limits the selection and use of air-purifying respirators.

1910.134(d)(1

General requirements.

1910.134(d)(1)(i)

The employer shall select and provide an appropriate respirator based on the respiratory hazard(s) to which the worker is exposed and workplace and user factors that affect respirator performance and reliability.

1910.134(d)(1)(ii)

The employer shall select a NIOSH-certified respirator. The respirator shall be used in compliance with the conditions of its certification.

1910.134(d)(1)(iii)

The employer shall identify and evaluate the respiratory hazard(s) in the workplace; this evaluation shall include a reasonable estimate of employee exposures to respiratory hazard(s) and an identification of the contaminant's chemical state and physical form. Where the employer cannot identify or reasonably estimate the employee exposure, the employer shall consider the atmosphere to be IDLH.

1910.134(d)(1)(iv)

The employer shall select respirators from a sufficient number of respirator models and sizes so that the respirator is acceptable to, and correctly fits, the user.

1910.134(d)(2)

Respirators for IDLH atmospheres.

1910.134(d)(2)(i)

The employer shall provide the following respirators for employee use in IDLH atmospheres:

1910.134(d)(2)(i)(A)

A full facepiece pressure demand SCBA certified by NIOSH for a minimum service life of thirty minutes, or

1910.134(d)(2)(i)(B)

A combination full facepiece pressure demand supplied-air respirator (SAR) with auxiliary self-contained air supply.

1910.134(d)(2)(ii)

Respirators provided only for escape from IDLH atmospheres shall be NIOSH-certified for escape from the atmosphere in which they will be used.

1910.134(d)(2)(iii)

All oxygen-deficient atmospheres shall be considered IDLH. Exception: If the employer demonstrates that, under all foreseeable conditions, the oxygen concentration can be maintained within the ranges specified in Table II of this section (i.e., for the altitudes set out in the table), then any atmosphere-supplying respirator may be used.

1910.134(d)(3)

Respirators for atmospheres that are not IDLH.

1910.134(d)(3)(i)

The employer shall provide a respirator that is adequate to protect the health of the employee and ensure compliance with all other OSHA statutory and regulatory requirements, under routine and reasonably foreseeable emergency situations.

1910.134(d)(3)(i)(A)

Assigned Protection Factors (APFs) Employers must use the assigned protection factors listed in Table I to select a respirator that meets or exceeds the required level of employee protection. When using a combination respirator (e.g., airline respirators with an air-purifying filter), employers must ensure that the assigned protection factor is appropriate to the mode of operation in which the respirator is being used.

Table I: Assigned Protection Factors[5]					
Type of Respirator[1,2]	Quarter mask	Half mask	Full facepiece	Helmet/Hood	Loose-fitting facepiece
1. Air-Purifying Respirator	5	10[3]	50	—	—
2. Powered Air-Purifying Respirator (PAPR)	—	50	1,000	25/1,000[4]	25
3. Supplied-Air Respirator (SAR) or Airline Respirator					
• Demand mode	—	10	50	—	—
• Continuous flow mode	—	50	1,000	25/1,000[4]	25
• Pressure-demand or other positive-pressure mode	—	50	1,000	—	—
4. Self-Contained Breathing Apparatus (SCBA)					
• Demand mode	—	10	50	50	—
• Pressure-demand or other positive-pressure mode (e.g., open/closed circuit)	—	—	10,000	10,000	—

Notes:

[1] Employers may select respirators assigned for use in higher workplace concentrations of a hazardous substance for use at lower concentrations of that substance, or when required respirator use is independent of concentration.

[2] The assigned protection factors in Table I are only effective when the employer implements a continuing, effective respirator program as required by this section (29 CFR 1910.134), including training, fit testing, maintenance, and use requirements.

[3] This APF category includes filtering facepieces, and half masks with elastomeric facepieces.

[4] The employer must have evidence provided by the respirator manufacturer that testing of these respirators demonstrates performance at a level of protection of 1,000 or greater to receive an APF of 1,000. This level of performance can best be demonstrated by performing a WPF or SWPF study or equivalent testing. Absent such testing, all other PAPRs and SARs with helmets/hoods are to be treated as loose-fitting facepiece respirators, and receive an APF of 25.

[5] These APFs do not apply to respirators used solely for escape. For escape respirators used in association with specific substances covered by 29 CFR 1910 subpart Z, employers must refer to the appropriate substance-specific standards in that subpart. Escape respirators for other IDLH atmospheres are specified by 29 CFR 1910.134(d)(2)(ii).

1910.134(d)(3)(i)(B)
Maximum Use Concentration (MUC)

1910.134(d)(3)(i)(B)(1)
The employer must select a respirator for employee use that maintains the employee's exposure to the hazardous substance, when measured outside the respirator, at or below the MUC.

1910.134(d)(3)(i)(B)(2)
Employers must not apply MUCs to conditions that are immediately dangerous to life or health (IDLH); instead, they must use respirators listed for IDLH conditions in paragraph (d)(2) of this standard.

1910.134(d)(3)(i)(B)(3)
When the calculated MUC exceeds the IDLH level for a hazardous substance, or the performance limits of the cartridge or canister, then employers must set the maximum MUC at that lower limit.

1910.134(d)(3)(ii)
The respirator selected shall be appropriate for the chemical state and physical form of the contaminant.

1910.134(d)(3)(iii)
For protection against gases and vapors, the employer shall provide:

1910.134(d)(3)(iii)(A)
An atmosphere-supplying respirator, or

1910.134(d)(3)(iii)(B)
An air-purifying respirator, provided that:

1910.134(d)(3)(iii)(B)(1)
The respirator is equipped with an end-of-service-life indicator (ESLI) certified by NIOSH for the contaminant; or

1910.134(d)(3)(iii)(B)(2)
If there is no ESLI appropriate for conditions in the employer's workplace, the employer implements a change schedule for canisters and cartridges that is based on objective information or data that will ensure that canisters and cartridges are changed before the end of their service life. The employer shall describe in the respirator program the information and data relied upon and the basis for the canister and

cartridge change schedule and the basis for reliance on the data.

1910.134(d)(3)(iv)
For protection against particulates, the employer shall provide:

1910.134(d)(3)(iv)(A)
An atmosphere-supplying respirator; or

1910.134(d)(3)(iv)(B)
An air-purifying respirator equipped with a filter certified by NIOSH under 30 CFR part 11 as a high efficiency particulate air (HEPA) filter, or an air-purifying respirator equipped with a filter certified for particulates by NIOSH under 42 CFR part 84; or

1910.134(d)(3)(iv)(C)
For contaminants consisting primarily of particles with mass median aerodynamic diameters (MMAD) of at least 2 micrometers, an air-purifying respirator equipped with any filter certified for particulates by NIOSH.

Table II: Oxygen Deficient Atmospheres	
Altitude (ft.)	Oxygen deficient atmospheres (% O_2) for which the employer may rely on atmosphere-supplying respirators
Less than 3,001	16.0-19.5
3,001-4,000	16.4-19.5
4,001-5,000	17.1-19.5
5,001-6,000	17.8-19.5
6,001-7,000	18.5-19.5
7,001-8,000[1]	19.3-19.5

[1] Above 8,000 feet the exception does not apply. Oxygen-enriched breathing air must be supplied above 14,000 feet.

1910.134(e)
Medical evaluation.
Using a respirator may place a physiological burden on employees that varies with the type of respirator worn, the job and workplace conditions in which the respirator is used, and the medical status of the employee. Accordingly, this paragraph specifies the minimum requirements for medical evaluation that employers must implement to determine the employee's ability to use a respirator.

1910.134(e)(1)
General. The employer shall provide a medical evaluation to determine the employee's ability to use a

respirator, before the employee is fit tested or required to use the respirator in the workplace. The employer may discontinue an employee's medical evaluations when the employee is no longer required to use a respirator.

1910.134(e)(2)
Medical evaluation procedures.

1910.134(e)(2)(i)
The employer shall identify a physician or other licensed health care professional (PLHCP) to perform medical evaluations using a medical questionnaire or an initial medical examination that obtains the same information as the medical questionnaire.

1910.134(e)(2)(ii)
The medical evaluation shall obtain the information requested by the questionnaire in Sections 1 and 2, Part A of Appendix C of this section.

1910.134(e)(3)
Follow-up medical examination.

1910.134(e)(3)(i)
The employer shall ensure that a follow-up medical examination is provided for an employee who gives a positive response to any question among questions 1 through 8 in Section 2, Part A of Appendix C or whose initial medical examination demonstrates the need for a follow-up medical examination.

1910.134(e)(3)(ii)
The follow-up medical examination shall include any medical tests, consultations, or diagnostic procedures that the PLHCP deems necessary to make a final determination.

1910.134(e)(4)
Administration of the medical questionnaire and examinations.

1910.134(e)(4)(i)
The medical questionnaire and examinations shall be administered confidentially during the employee's normal working hours or at a time and place convenient to the employee. The medical questionnaire shall be administered in a manner that ensures that the employee understands its content.

1910.134(e)(4)(ii)
The employer shall provide the employee with an opportunity to discuss the questionnaire and examination results with the PLHCP.

1910.134(e)(5)
Supplemental information for the PLHCP.

1910.134(e)(5)(i)
The following information must be provided to the PLHCP before the PLHCP makes a recommendation concerning an employee's ability to use a respirator:

1910.134(e)(5)(i)(A)
(A) The type and weight of the respirator to be used by the employee;

1910.134(e)(5)(i)(B)
The duration and frequency of respirator use (including use for rescue and escape);

1910.134(e)(5)(i)(C)
The expected physical work effort;

1910.134(e)(5)(i)(D)
Additional protective clothing and equipment to be worn; and

1910.134(e)(5)(i)(E)
Temperature and humidity extremes that may be encountered.

1910.134(e)(5)(ii)
Any supplemental information provided previously to the PLHCP regarding an employee need not be provided for a subsequent medical evaluation if the information and the PLHCP remain the same.

1910.134(e)(5)(iii)
The employer shall provide the PLHCP with a copy of the written respiratory protection program and a copy of this section.

Note to Paragraph (e)(5)(iii): When the employer replaces a PLHCP, the employer must ensure that the new PLHCP obtains this information, either by providing the documents directly to the PLHCP or having the documents transferred from the former PLHCP to the new PLHCP. However, OSHA does not expect employers to have employees medically reevaluated solely because a new PLHCP has been selected.

1910.134(e)(6)
Medical determination. In determining the employee's ability to use a respirator, the employer shall:

1910.134(e)(6)(i)
Obtain a written recommendation regarding the employee's ability to use the respirator from the PLHCP.

The recommendation shall provide only the following information:

1910.134(e)(6)(i)(A)
Any limitations on respirator use related to the medical condition of the employee, or relating to the workplace conditions in which the respirator will be used, including whether or not the employee is medically able to use the respirator;

1910.134(e)(6)(i)(B)
The need, if any, for follow-up medical evaluations; and

1910.134(e)(6)(i)(C)
A statement that the PLHCP has provided the employee with a copy of the PLHCP's written recommendation.

1910.134(e)(6)(ii)
If the respirator is a negative pressure respirator and the PLHCP finds a medical condition that may place the employee's health at increased risk if the respirator is used, the employer shall provide a PAPR if the PLHCP's medical evaluation finds that the employee can use such a respirator; if a subsequent medical evaluation finds that the employee is medically able to use a negative pressure respirator, then the employer is no longer required to provide a PAPR.

1910.134(e)(7)
Additional medical evaluations. At a minimum, the employer shall provide additional medical evaluations that comply with the requirements of this section if:

1910.134(e)(7)(i)
An employee reports medical signs or symptoms that are related to ability to use a respirator;

1910.134(e)(7)(ii)
A PLHCP, supervisor, or the respirator program administrator informs the employer that an employee needs to be reevaluated;

1910.134(e)(7)(iii)
Information from the respiratory protection program, including observations made during fit testing and program evaluation, indicates a need for employee reevaluation; or

1910.134(e)(7)(iv)
A change occurs in workplace conditions (e.g., physical work effort, protective clothing, temperature) that may result in a substantial increase in the physiological burden placed on an employee.

1910.134(f)
Fit testing.
This paragraph requires that, before an employee may be required to use any respirator with a negative or positive pressure tight-fitting facepiece, the employee must be fit tested with the same make, model, style, and size of respirator that will be used. This paragraph specifies the kinds of fit tests allowed, the procedures for conducting them, and how the results of the fit tests must be used.

1910.134(f)(1)
The employer shall ensure that employees using a tight-fitting facepiece respirator pass an appropriate qualitative fit test (QLFT) or quantitative fit test (QNFT) as stated in this paragraph.

1910.134(f)(2)
The employer shall ensure that an employee using a tight-fitting facepiece respirator is fit tested prior to initial use of the respirator, whenever a different respirator facepiece (size, style, model or make) is used, and at least annually thereafter.

1910.134(f)(3)
The employer shall conduct an additional fit test whenever the employee reports, or the employer, PLHCP, supervisor, or program administrator makes visual observations of, changes in the employee's physical condition that could affect respirator fit. Such conditions include, but are not limited to, facial scarring, dental changes, cosmetic surgery, or an obvious change in body weight.

1910.134(f)(4)
If after passing a QLFT or QNFT, the employee subsequently notifies the employer, program administrator, supervisor, or PLHCP that the fit of the respirator is unacceptable, the employee shall be given a reasonable opportunity to select a different respirator facepiece and to be retested.

1910.134(f)(5)
The fit test shall be administered using an OSHA-accepted QLFT or QNFT protocol. The OSHA-accepted QLFT and QNFT protocols and procedures are contained in Appendix A of this section.

1910.134(f)(6)
QLFT may only be used to fit test negative pressure air-purifying respirators that must achieve a fit factor of 100 or less.

1910.134(f)(7)
If the fit factor, as determined through an OSHA-accepted QNFT protocol, is equal to or greater than 100 for tight-fitting half facepieces, or equal to or greater than 500 for tight-fitting full facepieces, the QNFT has been passed with that respirator.

1910.134(f)(8)
Fit testing of tight-fitting atmosphere-supplying respirators and tight-fitting powered air-purifying respirators shall be accomplished by performing quantitative or qualitative fit testing in the negative pressure mode, regardless of the mode of operation (negative or positive pressure) that is used for respiratory protection.

1910.134(f)(8)(i)
Qualitative fit testing of these respirators shall be accomplished by temporarily converting the respirator user's actual facepiece into a negative pressure respirator with appropriate filters, or by using an identical negative pressure air-purifying respirator facepiece with the same sealing surfaces as a surrogate for the atmosphere-supplying or powered air-purifying respirator facepiece.

1910.134(f)(8)(ii)
Quantitative fit testing of these respirators shall be accomplished by modifying the facepiece to allow sampling inside the facepiece in the breathing zone of the user, midway between the nose and mouth. This requirement shall be accomplished by installing a permanent sampling probe onto a surrogate facepiece, or by using a sampling adapter designed to temporarily provide a means of sampling air from inside the facepiece.

1910.134(f)(8)(iii)
Any modifications to the respirator facepiece for fit testing shall be completely removed, and the facepiece restored to NIOSH-approved configuration, before that facepiece can be used in the workplace.

1910.134(g)
Use of respirators.
This paragraph requires employers to establish and implement procedures for the proper use of respirators. These requirements include prohibiting conditions that may result in facepiece seal leakage, preventing employees from removing respirators in hazardous environments, taking actions to ensure continued effective respirator operation throughout the work shift, and establishing procedures for the use of respirators in IDLH atmospheres or in interior structural firefighting situations.

1910.134(g)(1)
Facepiece seal protection.
1910.134(g)(1)(i)
The employer shall not permit respirators with tight-fitting facepieces to be worn by employees who have:

1910.134(g)(1)(i)(A)
Facial hair that comes between the sealing surface of the facepiece and the face or that interferes with valve function; or

1910.134(g)(1)(i)(B)
Any condition that interferes with the face-to-facepiece seal or valve function.

1910.134(g)(1)(ii)
If an employee wears corrective glasses or goggles or other personal protective equipment, the employer shall ensure that such equipment is worn in a manner that does not interfere with the seal of the facepiece to the face of the user.

1910.134(g)(1)(iii)
For all tight-fitting respirators, the employer shall ensure that employees perform a user seal check each time they put on the respirator using the procedures in Appendix B-1 or procedures recommended by the respirator manufacturer that the employer demonstrates are as effective as those in Appendix B-1 of this section.

1910.134(g)(2)
Continuing respirator effectiveness.
1910.134(g)(2)(i)
Appropriate surveillance shall be maintained of work area conditions and degree of employee exposure or stress. When there is a change in work area conditions or degree of employee exposure or stress that may affect respirator effectiveness, the employer shall reevaluate the continued effectiveness of the respirator.

1910.134(g)(2)(ii)
The employer shall ensure that employees leave the respirator use area:

1910.134(g)(2)(ii)(A)
To wash their faces and respirator facepieces as necessary to prevent eye or skin irritation associated with respirator use; or

1910.134(g)(2)(ii)(B)
If they detect vapor or gas breakthrough, changes in breathing resistance, or leakage of the facepiece; or

1910.134(g)(2)(ii)(C)
To replace the respirator or the filter, cartridge, or canister elements.

1910.134(g)(2)(iii)
If the employee detects vapor or gas breakthrough, changes in breathing resistance, or leakage of the facepiece, the employer must replace or repair the respirator before allowing the employee to return to the work area.

1910.134(g)(3)
Procedures for IDLH atmospheres. For all IDLH atmospheres, the employer shall ensure that:

1910.134(g)(3)(i)
One employee or, when needed, more than one employee is located outside the IDLH atmosphere;

1910.134(g)(3)(ii)
Visual, voice, or signal line communication is maintained between the employee(s) in the IDLH atmosphere and the employee(s) located outside the IDLH atmosphere;

1910.134(g)(3)(iii)
The employee(s) located outside the IDLH atmosphere are trained and equipped to provide effective emergency rescue;

1910.134(g)(3)(iv)
The employer or designee is notified before the employee(s) located outside the IDLH atmosphere enter the IDLH atmosphere to provide emergency rescue;

1910.134(g)(3)(v)
The employer or designee authorized to do so by the employer, once notified, provides necessary assistance appropriate to the situation;

1910.134(g)(3)(vi)
Employee(s) located outside the IDLH atmospheres are equipped with:

1910.134(g)(3)(vi)(A)
Pressure demand or other positive pressure SCBAs, or a pressure demand or other positive pressure supplied-air respirator with auxiliary SCBA; and either

1910.134(g)(3)(vi)(B)
Appropriate retrieval equipment for removing the employee(s) who enter(s) these hazardous atmospheres where retrieval equipment would contribute to the rescue of the employee(s) and would not increase the overall risk resulting from entry; or

1910.134(g)(3)(vi)(C)
Equivalent means for rescue where retrieval equipment is not required under paragraph (g)(3)(vi)(B).

1910.134(g)(4)
Procedures for interior structural firefighting. In addition to the requirements set forth under paragraph (g)(3), in interior structural fires, the employer shall ensure that:

1910.134(g)(4)(i)
At least two employees enter the IDLH atmosphere and remain in visual or voice contact with one another at all times;

1910.134(g)(4)(ii)
At least two employees are located outside the IDLH atmosphere; and

1910.134(g)(4)(iii)
All employees engaged in interior structural firefighting use SCBAs.

Note 1 to paragraph (g): One of the two individuals located outside the IDLH atmosphere may be assigned to an additional role, such as incident commander in charge of the emergency or safety officer, so long as this individual is able to perform assistance or rescue activities without jeopardizing the safety or health of any firefighter working at the incident.

Note 2 to paragraph (g): Nothing in this section is meant to preclude firefighters from performing emergency rescue activities before an entire team has assembled.

1910.134(h)
Maintenance and care of respirators.
This paragraph requires the employer to provide for the cleaning and disinfecting, storage, inspection, and repair of respirators used by employees.

1910.134(h)(1)
Cleaning and disinfecting. The employer shall provide each respirator user with a respirator that is clean, sanitary, and in good working order. The employer shall ensure that respirators are cleaned and disinfected using the procedures in Appendix B-2 of this section, or procedures recommended by the respirator manufacturer, provided that such procedures are of equivalent effectiveness. The respirators shall be cleaned and disinfected at the following intervals:

1910.134(h)(1)(i)
Respirators issued for the exclusive use of an employee shall be cleaned and disinfected as often as necessary to be maintained in a sanitary condition;

1910.134(h)(1)(ii)
Respirators issued to more than one employee shall be cleaned and disinfected before being worn by different individuals;

1910.134(h)(1)(iii)
Respirators maintained for emergency use shall be cleaned and disinfected after each use; and

1910.134(h)(1)(iv)
Respirators used in fit testing and training shall be cleaned and disinfected after each use.

1910.134(h)(2)
Storage. The employer shall ensure that respirators are stored as follows:

1910.134(h)(2)(i)
All respirators shall be stored to protect them from damage, contamination, dust, sunlight, extreme temperatures, excessive moisture, and damaging chemicals, and they shall be packed or stored to prevent deformation of the facepiece and exhalation valve.

1910.134(h)(2)(ii)
In addition to the requirements of paragraph (h)(2)(i) of this section, emergency respirators shall be:

1910.134(h)(2)(ii)(A)
Kept accessible to the work area;

1910.134(h)(2)(ii)(B)
Stored in compartments or in covers that are clearly marked as containing emergency respirators; and

1910.134(h)(2)(ii)(C)
Stored in accordance with any applicable manufacturer instructions.

1910.134(h)(3)
Inspection.

1910.134(h)(3)(i)
The employer shall ensure that respirators are inspected as follows:

1910.134(h)(3)(i)(A)
All respirators used in routine situations shall be inspected before each use and during cleaning;

1910.134(h)(3)(i)(B)
All respirators maintained for use in emergency situations shall be inspected at least monthly and in accordance with the manufacturer's recommendations, and shall be checked for proper function before and after each use; and

1910.134(h)(3)(i)(C)
Emergency escape-only respirators shall be inspected before being carried into the workplace for use.

1910.134(h)(3)(ii)
The employer shall ensure that respirator inspections include the following:

1910.134(h)(3)(ii)(A)

A check of respirator function, tightness of connections, and the condition of the various parts including, but not limited to, the facepiece, head straps, valves, connecting tube, and cartridges, canisters or filters; and

1910.134(h)(3)(ii)(B)

A check of elastomeric parts for pliability and signs of deterioration.

1910.134(h)(3)(iii)

In addition to the requirements of paragraphs (h)(3)(i) and (ii) of this section, self-contained breathing apparatus shall be inspected monthly. Air and oxygen cylinders shall be maintained in a fully charged state and shall be recharged when the pressure falls to 90% of the manufacturer's recommended pressure level. The employer shall determine that the regulator and warning devices function properly.

1910.134(h)(3)(iv)

For respirators maintained for emergency use, the employer shall:

1910.134(h)(3)(iv)(A)

Certify the respirator by documenting the date the inspection was performed, the name (or signature) of the person who made the inspection, the findings, required remedial action, and a serial number or other means of identifying the inspected respirator; and

1910.134(h)(3)(iv)(B)

Provide this information on a tag or label that is attached to the storage compartment for the respirator, is kept with the respirator, or is included in inspection reports stored as paper or electronic files. This information shall be maintained until replaced following a subsequent certification.

1910.134(h)(4)

Repairs. The employer shall ensure that respirators that fail an inspection or are otherwise found to be defective are removed from service, and are discarded or repaired or adjusted in accordance with the following procedures:

1910.134(h)(4)(i)

Repairs or adjustments to respirators are to be made only by persons appropriately trained to perform such operations and shall use only the respirator manufacturer's NIOSH-approved parts designed for the respirator;

1910.134(h)(4)(ii)

Repairs shall be made according to the manufacturer's recommendations and specifications for the type and extent of repairs to be performed; and

1910.134(h)(4)(iii)

Reducing and admission valves, regulators, and alarms shall be adjusted or repaired only by the manufacturer or a technician trained by the manufacturer.

1910.134(i)

Breathing air quality and use.

This paragraph requires the employer to provide employees using atmosphere-supplying respirators (supplied-air and SCBA) with breathing gases of high purity.

1910.134(i)(1)

The employer shall ensure that compressed air, compressed oxygen, liquid air, and liquid oxygen used for respiration accords with the following specifications:

1910.134(i)(1)(i)

Compressed and liquid oxygen shall meet the United States Pharmacopoeia requirements for medical or breathing oxygen; and

1910.134(i)(1)(ii)

Compressed breathing air shall meet at least the requirements for Grade D breathing air described in ANSI/Compressed Gas Association Commodity Specification for Air, G-7.1-1989, to include:

1910.134(i)(1)(ii)(A)

Oxygen content (v/v) of 19.5-23.5%;

1910.134(i)(1)(ii)(B)

Hydrocarbon (condensed) content of 5 milligrams per cubic meter of air or less;

1910.134(i)(1)(ii)(C)

Carbon monoxide (CO) content of 10 ppm or less;

1910.134(i)(1)(ii)(D)

Carbon dioxide content of 1,000 ppm or less; and

1910.134(i)(1)(ii)(E)

Lack of noticeable odor.

1910.134(i)(2)

The employer shall ensure that compressed oxygen is not used in atmosphere-supplying respirators that have previously used compressed air.

1910.134(i)(3)

The employer shall ensure that oxygen concentrations greater than 23.5% are used only in equipment designed for oxygen service or distribution.

1910.134(i)(4)

The employer shall ensure that cylinders used to supply breathing air to respirators meet the following requirements:

1910.134(i)(4)(i)

Cylinders are tested and maintained as prescribed in the Shipping Container Specification Regulations of the Department of Transportation (49 CFR part 173 and part 178);

1910.134(i)(4)(ii)

Cylinders of purchased breathing air have a certificate of analysis from the supplier that the breathing air meets the requirements for Grade D breathing air; and

1910.134(i)(4)(iii)

The moisture content in the cylinder does not exceed a dew point of -50 deg.F (-45.6 deg.C) at 1 atmosphere pressure.

1910.134(i)(5)

The employer shall ensure that compressors used to supply breathing air to respirators are constructed and situated so as to:

1910.134(i)(5)(i)

Prevent entry of contaminated air into the air-supply system;

1910.134(i)(5)(ii)

Minimize moisture content so that the dew point at 1 atmosphere pressure is 10 degrees F (5.56 deg.C) below the ambient temperature;

1910.134(i)(5)(iii)

Have suitable in-line air-purifying sorbent beds and filters to further ensure breathing air quality. Sorbent beds and filters shall be maintained and replaced or refurbished periodically following the manufacturer's instructions.

1910.134(i)(5)(iv)

Have a tag containing the most recent change date and the signature of the person authorized by the employer to perform the change. The tag shall be maintained at the compressor.

1910.134(i)(6)

For compressors that are not oil-lubricated, the em-

ployer shall ensure that carbon monoxide levels in the breathing air do not exceed 10 ppm.

1910.134(i)(7)

For oil-lubricated compressors, the employer shall use a high-temperature or carbon monoxide alarm, or both, to monitor carbon monoxide levels. If only high-temperature alarms are used, the air supply shall be monitored at intervals sufficient to prevent carbon monoxide in the breathing air from exceeding 10 ppm.

1910.134(i)(8)

The employer shall ensure that breathing air couplings are incompatible with outlets for nonrespirable worksite air or other gas systems. No asphyxiating substance shall be introduced into breathing air lines.

1910.134(i)(9)

The employer shall use breathing gas containers marked in accordance with the NIOSH respirator certification standard, 42 CFR part 84.

1910.134(j)

Identification of filters, cartridges, and canisters.

The employer shall ensure that all filters, cartridges and canisters used in the workplace are labeled and color coded with the NIOSH approval label and that the label is not removed and remains legible.

1910.134(k)

Training and information.

This paragraph requires the employer to provide effective training to employees who are required to use respirators. The training must be comprehensive, understandable, and recur annually, and more often if necessary. This paragraph also requires the employer to provide the basic information on respirators in Appendix D of this section to employees who wear respirators when not required by this section or by the employer to do so.

1910.134(k)(1)

The employer shall ensure that each employee can demonstrate knowledge of at least the following:

1910.134(k)(1)(i)

Why the respirator is necessary and how improper fit, usage, or maintenance can compromise the protective effect of the respirator;

1910.134(k)(1)(ii)

What the limitations and capabilities of the respirator are;

1910.134(k)(1)(iii)

How to use the respirator effectively in emergency situations, including situations in which the respirator malfunctions;

1910.134(k)(1)(iv)

How to inspect, put on and remove, use, and check the seals of the respirator;

1910.134(k)(1)(v)

What the procedures are for maintenance and storage of the respirator;

1910.134(k)(1)(vi)

How to recognize medical signs and symptoms that may limit or prevent the effective use of respirators; and

1910.134(k)(1)(vii)

The general requirements of this section.

1910.134(k)(2)

The training shall be conducted in a manner that is understandable to the employee.

1910.134(k)(3)

The employer shall provide the training prior to requiring the employee to use a respirator in the workplace.

1910.134(k)(4)

An employer who is able to demonstrate that a new employee has received training within the last 12 months that addresses the elements specified in paragraph (k)(1)(i) through (vii) is not required to repeat such training provided that, as required by paragraph (k)(1), the employee can demonstrate knowledge of those element(s). Previous training not repeated initially by the employer must be provided no later than 12 months from the date of the previous training.

1910.134(k)(5)

Retraining shall be administered annually, and when the following situations occur:

1910.134(k)(5)(i)

Changes in the workplace or the type of respirator render previous training obsolete;

1910.134(k)(5)(ii)

Inadequacies in the employee's knowledge or use of the respirator indicate that the employee has not retained the requisite understanding or skill; or

1910.134(k)(5)(iii)

Any other situation arises in which retraining appears necessary to ensure safe respirator use.

1910.134(k)(6)

The basic advisory information on respirators, as presented in Appendix D of this section, shall be provided by the employer in any written or oral format, to employees who wear respirators when such use is not required by this section or by the employer.

1910.134(l)
Program evaluation.

This section requires the employer to conduct evaluations of the workplace to ensure that the written respiratory protection program is being properly implemented, and to consult employees to ensure that they are using the respirators properly.

1910.134(l)(1)

The employer shall conduct evaluations of the workplace as necessary to ensure that the provisions of the current written program are being effectively implemented and that it continues to be effective.

1910.134(l)(2)

The employer shall regularly consult employees required to use respirators to assess the employees' views on program effectiveness and to identify any problems. Any problems that are identified during this assessment shall be corrected. Factors to be assessed include, but are not limited to:

1910.134(l)(2)(i)

Respirator fit (including the ability to use the respirator without interfering with effective workplace performance);

1910.134(l)(2)(ii)

Appropriate respirator selection for the hazards to which the employee is exposed;

1910.134(l)(2)(iii)

Proper respirator use under the workplace conditions the employee encounters; and

1910.134(l)(2)(iv)

Proper respirator maintenance.

1910.134(m)
Recordkeeping.

This section requires the employer to establish and retain written information regarding medical evaluations, fit testing, and the respirator program. This information will facilitate employee involvement in the respirator program, assist the employer in auditing the adequacy of the program, and provide a record for compliance determinations by OSHA.

1910.134(m)(1)
Medical evaluation. Records of medical evaluations required by this section must be retained and made available in accordance with 29 CFR 1910.1020.

1910.134(m)(2)
Fit testing.

1910.134(m)(2)(i)
The employer shall establish a record of the qualitative and quantitative fit tests administered to an employee including:

1910.134(m)(2)(i)(A)
The name or identification of the employee tested;

1910.134(m)(2)(i)(B)
Type of fit test performed;

1910.134(m)(2)(i)(C)
Specific make, model, style, and size of respirator tested;

1910.134(m)(2)(i)(D)
Date of test; and

1910.134(m)(2)(i)(E)
The pass/fail results for QLFTs or the fit factor and strip chart recording or other recording of the test results for QNFTs.

1910.134(m)(2)(ii)
Fit test records shall be retained for respirator users until the next fit test is administered.

1910.134(m)(3)
A written copy of the current respirator program shall be retained by the employer.

1910.134(m)(4)
Written materials required to be retained under this paragraph shall be made available upon request to affected employees and to the Assistant Secretary or designee for examination and copying.

1910.134(n)
Effective date.
Paragraphs (d)(3)(i)(A) and (d)(3)(i)(B) of this section become effective November 22, 2006.

1910.134(o)
Appendices.

1910.134(o)(1)
Compliance with Appendix A, Appendix B-1, Appendix B-2, and Appendix C of this section is mandatory.

1910.134(o)(2)
Appendix D of this section is non-mandatory and is not intended to create any additional obligations not otherwise imposed or to detract from any existing obligations.

[63 FR 1152, Jan. 8, 1998; 63 FR 20098, April 23, 1998; 71 FR 16672, April 3, 2006; 71 FR 50187, August 24, 2006]

Appendix A to §1910.134:
Fit Testing Procedures (Mandatory)

Part I. OSHA-Accepted Fit Test Protocols

A. Fit Testing Procedures -- General Requirements

The employer shall conduct fit testing using the following procedures. The requirements in this appendix apply to all OSHA-accepted fit test methods, both QLFT and QNFT.

1. The test subject shall be allowed to pick the most acceptable respirator from a sufficient number of respirator models and sizes so that the respirator is acceptable to, and correctly fits, the user.

2. Prior to the selection process, the test subject shall be shown how to put on a respirator, how it should be positioned on the face, how to set strap tension and how to determine an acceptable fit. A mirror shall be available to assist the subject in evaluating the fit and positioning of the respirator. This instruction may not constitute the subject's formal training on respirator use, because it is only a review.

3. The test subject shall be informed that he/she is being asked to select the respirator that provides the most acceptable fit. Each respirator represents a different size and shape, and if fitted and used properly, will provide adequate protection.

4. The test subject shall be instructed to hold each chosen facepiece up to the face and eliminate those that obviously do not give an acceptable fit.

5. The more acceptable facepieces are noted in case the one selected proves unacceptable; the most comfortable mask is donned and worn at least five minutes to assess comfort. Assistance in assessing comfort can be given by discussing the points in the following item A.6. If the test subject is not familiar with using a particular respirator, the test subject shall be directed to don the mask several times and to adjust the straps each time to become adept at setting proper tension on the straps.

6. Assessment of comfort shall include a review of the following points with the test subject and allowing the test subject adequate time to determine the comfort of the respirator:
   (a) Position of the mask on the nose
   (b) Room for eye protection
   (c) Room to talk
   (d) Position of mask on face and cheeks

7. The following criteria shall be used to help determine the adequacy of the respirator fit:
   (a) Chin properly placed;
   (b) Adequate strap tension, not overly tightened;
   (c) Fit across nose bridge;
   (d) Respirator of proper size to span distance from nose to chin;
   (e) Tendency of respirator to slip;
   (f) Self-observation in mirror to evaluate fit and respirator position.

8. The test subject shall conduct a user seal check, either the negative and positive pressure seal checks described in Appendix B-1 of this section or those recommended by the respirator manufacturer which provide equivalent protection to the procedures in Appendix B-1. Before conducting the negative and positive pressure checks, the subject shall be told to seat the mask on the face by moving the head from side-to-side and up and down slowly while taking in a few slow deep breaths. Another facepiece shall be selected and retested if the test subject fails the user seal check tests.

9. The test shall not be conducted if there is any hair growth between the skin and the facepiece sealing surface, such as stubble beard growth, beard, mustache or sideburns which cross the respirator sealing surface. Any type of apparel which interferes with a satisfactory fit shall be altered or removed.

10. If a test subject exhibits difficulty in breathing during the tests, she or he shall be referred to a physician or other licensed health care professional, as appropriate, to determine whether the test subject can wear a respirator while performing her or his duties.

11. If the employee finds the fit of the respirator unacceptable, the test subject shall be given the opportunity to select a different respirator and to be retested.

12. Exercise regimen. Prior to the commencement of the fit test, the test subject shall be given a description of the fit test and the test subject's responsibilities during the test procedure. The description of the process shall include a description of the test exercises that the subject will be performing. The respirator to be tested shall be worn for at least 5 minutes before the start of the fit test.

13. The fit test shall be performed while the test subject is wearing any applicable safety equipment that may be worn during actual respirator use which could interfere with respirator fit.

14. Test Exercises.

(a) Employers must perform the following test exercises for all fit testing methods prescribed in this appendix, except for the CNP quantitative fit testing protocol and the CNP REDON quantitative fit testing protocol. For these two protocols, employers must ensure that the test subjects (i.e., employees) perform the exercise procedure specified in Part I.C.4(b) of this appendix for the CNP quantitative fit testing protocol, or the exercise procedure described in Part I.C.5(b) of this appendix for the CNP REDON quantitative fit-testing protocol. For the remaining fit testing methods, employers must ensure that employees perform the test exercises in the appropriate test environment in the following manner:

(1) Normal breathing. In a normal standing position, without talking, the subject shall breathe normally.

(2) Deep breathing. In a normal standing position, the subject shall breathe slowly and deeply, taking caution so as not to hyperventilate.

(3) Turning head side to side. Standing in place, the subject shall slowly turn his/her head from side to side between the extreme positions on each side. The head shall be held at each extreme momentarily so the subject can inhale at each side.

(4) Moving head up and down. Standing in place, the subject shall slowly move his/her head up and down. The subject shall be instructed to inhale in the up position (i.e., when looking toward the ceiling).

(5) Talking. The subject shall talk out loud slowly and loud enough so as to be heard clearly by the test conductor. The subject can read from a prepared text such as the Rainbow Passage, count backward from 100, or recite a memorized poem or song.

Rainbow Passage

When the sunlight strikes raindrops in the air, they act like a prism and form a rainbow. The rainbow is a division of white light into many beautiful colors. These take the shape of a long round arch, with its path high above, and its two ends apparently beyond the horizon. There is, according to legend, a boiling pot of gold at one end. People look, but no one ever finds it. When a man looks for something beyond reach, his friends say he is looking for the pot of gold at the end of the rainbow.

(6) Grimace. The test subject shall grimace by smiling or frowning. (This applies only to QNFT testing; it is not performed for QLFT)

(7) Bending over. The test subject shall bend at the waist as if he/she were to touch his/her toes. Jogging in place shall be substituted for this exercise in those test environments such as shroud type QNFT or QLFT units that do not permit bending over at the waist.

(8) Normal breathing. Same as exercise (1).

(b) Each test exercise shall be performed for one minute except for the grimace exercise which shall be performed for 15 seconds. The test subject shall be questioned by the test conductor regarding the comfort of the respirator upon completion of the protocol. If it has become unacceptable, another model of respirator shall be tried. The respirator shall not be adjusted once the fit test exercises begin. Any adjustment voids the test, and the fit test must be repeated.

B. Qualitative Fit Test (QLFT) Protocols

1. General

(a) The employer shall ensure that persons administering QLFT are able to prepare test solutions, calibrate equipment and perform tests properly, recognize invalid tests, and ensure that test equipment is in proper working order.

(b) The employer shall ensure that QLFT equipment is kept clean and well maintained so as to operate within the parameters for which it was designed.

2. Isoamyl Acetate Protocol

Note: This protocol is not appropriate to use for the fit testing of particulate respirators. If used to fit test particulate respirators, the respirator must be equipped with an organic vapor filter.

(a) Odor Threshold Screening

Odor threshold screening, performed without wearing a respirator, is intended to determine if the individual tested can detect the odor of isoamyl acetate at low levels.

(1) Three 1 liter glass jars with metal lids are required.

(2) Odor-free water (e.g., distilled or spring water) at approximately 25 deg. C (77 deg. F) shall be used for the solutions.

(3) The isoamyl acetate (IAA) (also known a3 isopentyl acetate) stock solution is prepared by adding 1 ml of pure IAA to 800 ml of odor-free water in a 1 liter jar, closing the lid and shaking for 30 seconds. A new solution shall be prepared at least weekly.

(4) The screening test shall be conducted in a room separate from the room used for actual fit testing. The two rooms shall be well-ventilated to prevent the odor of IAA from becoming evident in the general room air where testing takes place.

(5) The odor test solution is prepared in a second jar by placing 0.4 ml of the stock solution into 500 ml of odor-free water using a clean dropper or pipette. The solution shall be shaken for 30 seconds and allowed to stand for two to three minutes so that the IAA concentration above the liquid may reach equilibrium. This solution shall be used for only one day.

(6) A test blank shall be prepared in a third jar by adding 500 cc of odor-free water.

(7) The odor test and test blank jar lids shall be labeled (e.g., 1 and 2) for jar identification. Labels shall be placed on the lids so that they can be peeled off periodically and switched to maintain the integrity of the test.

(8) The following instruction shall be typed on a card and placed on the table in front of the two test jars (i.e., 1 and 2): "The purpose of this test is to determine if you can smell banana oil at a low concentration. The two bottles in front of you contain water. One of these bottles also contains a small amount of banana oil. Be sure the covers are on tight, then shake each bottle for two seconds. Unscrew the lid of each bottle, one at a time, and sniff at the mouth of the bottle. Indicate to the test conductor which bottle contains banana oil."

(9) The mixtures used in the IAA odor detection test shall be prepared in an area separate from where the test is performed, in order to prevent olfactory fatigue in the subject.

(10) If the test subject is unable to correctly identify the jar containing the odor test solution, the IAA qualitative fit test shall not be performed.

(11) If the test subject correctly identifies the jar containing the odor test solution, the test subject may proceed to respirator selection and fit testing.

(b) Isoamyl Acetate Fit Test

(1) The fit test chamber shall be a clear 55-gallon drum liner suspended inverted over a 2-foot diameter frame so that the top of the chamber is about 6 inches above the test subject's head. If no drum liner is available, a similar chamber shall be constructed using plastic sheeting. The inside top center of the chamber shall have a small hook attached.

(2) Each respirator used for the fitting and fit testing shall be equipped with organic vapor cartridges or offer protection against organic vapors.

(3) After selecting, donning, and properly adjusting a respirator, the test subject shall wear it to the fit testing room. This room shall be separate from the room used for odor threshold screening and respirator selection, and shall be well-ventilated, as by an exhaust fan or lab hood, to prevent general room contamination.

(4) A copy of the test exercises and any prepared text from which the subject is to read shall be taped to the inside of the test chamber.

(5) Upon entering the test chamber, the test subject shall be given a 6-inch by 5-inch piece of paper towel, or other porous, absorbent, singleply material, folded in half and wetted with 0.75 ml of pure IAA. The test subject shall hang the wet towel on the hook at the top of the chamber. An IAA test swab or ampule may be substituted for the IAA wetted paper towel provided it has been demonstrated that the alternative IAA source will generate an IAA test atmosphere with a concentration equivalent to that generated by the paper towel method.

(6) Allow two minutes for the IAA test concentration to stabilize before starting the fit test exercises. This would be an appropriate time to talk with the test subject; to explain the fit test, the importance of his/her cooperation, and the purpose for the test exercises; or to demonstrate some of the exercises.

(7) If at any time during the test, the subject detects the banana-like odor of IAA, the test is failed. The subject shall quickly exit from the

test chamber and leave the test area to avoid olfactory fatigue.

(8) If the test is failed, the subject shall return to the selection room and remove the respirator. The test subject shall repeat the odor sensitivity test, select and put on another respirator, return to the test area and again begin the fit test procedure described in (b) (1) through (7) above. The process continues until a respirator that fits well has been found. Should the odor sensitivity test be failed, the subject shall wait at least 5 minutes before retesting. Odor sensitivity will usually have returned by this time.

(9) If the subject passes the test, the efficiency of the test procedure shall be demonstrated by having the subject break the respirator face seal and take a breath before exiting the chamber.

(10) When the test subject leaves the chamber, the subject shall remove the saturated towel and return it to the person conducting the test, so that there is no significant IAA concentration buildup in the chamber during subsequent tests. The used towels shall be kept in a self-sealing plastic bag to keep the test area from being contaminated.

3. Saccharin Solution Aerosol Protocol

The entire screening and testing procedure shall be explained to the test subject prior to the conduct of the screening test.

(a) Taste threshold screening. The saccharin taste threshold screening, performed without wearing a respirator, is intended to determine whether the individual being tested can detect the taste of saccharin.

(1) During threshold screening as well as during fit testing, subjects shall wear an enclosure about the head and shoulders that is approximately 12 inches in diameter by 14 inches tall with at least the front portion clear and that allows free movements of the head when a respirator is worn. An enclosure substantially similar to the 3M hood assembly, parts # FT 14 and # FT 15 combined, is adequate.

(2) The test enclosure shall have a 3/4-inch (1.9 cm) hole in front of the test subject's nose and mouth area to accommodate the nebulizer nozzle.

(3) The test subject shall don the test enclosure. Throughout the threshold screening test, the test subject shall breathe through his/her slightly open mouth with tongue extended. The subject is instructed to report when he/she detects a sweet taste.

(4) Using a DeVilbiss Model 40 Inhalation Medication Nebulizer or equivalent, the test conductor shall spray the threshold check solution into the enclosure. The nozzle is directed away from the nose and mouth of the person. This nebulizer shall be clearly marked to distinguish it from the fit test solution nebulizer.

(5) The threshold check solution is prepared by dissolving 0.83 gram of sodium saccharin USP in 100 ml of warm water. It can be prepared by putting 1 ml of the fit test solution (see (b)(5) below) in 100 ml of distilled water.

(6) To produce the aerosol, the nebulizer bulb is firmly squeezed so that it collapses completely, then released and allowed to fully expand.

(7) Ten squeezes are repeated rapidly and then the test subject is asked whether the saccharin can be tasted. If the test subject reports tasting the sweet taste during the ten squeezes, the screening test is completed. The taste threshold is noted as ten regardless of the number of squeezes actually completed.

(8) If the first response is negative, ten more squeezes are repeated rapidly and the test subject is again asked whether the saccharin is tasted. If the test subject reports tasting the sweet taste during the second ten squeezes, the screening test is completed. The taste threshold is noted as twenty regardless of the number of squeezes actually completed.

(9) If the second response is negative, ten more squeezes are repeated rapidly and the test subject is again asked whether the saccharin is tasted. If the test subject reports tasting the sweet taste during the third set of ten squeezes, the screening test is completed. The taste threshold is noted as thirty regardless of the number of squeezes actually completed.

(10) The test conductor will take note of the number of squeezes required to solicit a taste response.

(11) If the saccharin is not tasted after 30 squeezes (step 10), the test subject is unable to taste saccharin and may not perform the saccharin fit test.

Note to paragraph 3. (a): If the test subject eats or drinks something sweet before the screening test, he/she may be unable to taste the weak saccharin solution.

(12) If a taste response is elicited, the test subject shall be asked to take note of the taste for reference in the fit test.

(13) Correct use of the nebulizer means that approximately 1 ml of liquid is used at a time in the nebulizer body.

(14) The nebulizer shall be thoroughly rinsed in water, shaken dry, and refilled at least each morning and afternoon or at least every four hours.

(b) Saccharin solution aerosol fit test procedure.

(1) The test subject may not eat, drink (except plain water), smoke, or chew gum for 15 minutes before the test.

(2) The fit test uses the same enclosure described in 3. (a) above.

(3) The test subject shall don the enclosure while wearing the respirator selected in section I. A. of this appendix. The respirator shall be properly adjusted and equipped with a particulate filter(s).

(4) A second DeVilbiss Model 40 Inhalation Medication Nebulizer or equivalent is used to spray the fit test solution into the enclosure. This nebulizer shall be clearly marked to distinguish it from the screening test solution nebulizer.

(5) The fit test solution is prepared by adding 83 grams of sodium saccharin to 100 ml of warm water.

(6) As before, the test subject shall breathe through the slightly open mouth with tongue extended, and report if he/she tastes the sweet taste of saccharin.

(7) The nebulizer is inserted into the hole in the front of the enclosure and an initial concentration of saccharin fit test solution is sprayed into the enclosure using the same number of squeezes (either 10, 20 or 30 squeezes) based on the number of squeezes required to elicit a taste response as noted during the screening test. A minimum of 10 squeezes is required.

(8) After generating the aerosol, the test subject shall be instructed to perform the exercises in section I. A. 14. of this appendix.

(9) Every 30 seconds the aerosol concentration shall be replenished using one half the original number of squeezes used initially (e.g., 5, 10 or 15).

(10) The test subject shall indicate to the test conductor if at any time during the fit test the taste of saccharin is detected. If the test subject does not report tasting the saccharin, the test is passed.

(11) If the taste of saccharin is detected, the fit is deemed unsatisfactory and the test is failed. A different respirator shall be tried and the entire test procedure is repeated (taste threshold screening and fit testing).

(12) Since the nebulizer has a tendency to clog during use, the test operator must make periodic checks of the nebulizer to ensure that it is not clogged. If clogging is found at the end of the test session, the test is invalid.

4. BitrexTM (Denatonium Benzoate) Solution Aerosol Qualitative Fit Test Protocol

The BitrexTM (Denatonium benzoate) solution aerosol QLFT protocol uses the published saccharin test protocol because that protocol is widely accepted. Bitrex is routinely used as a taste aversion agent in household liquids which children should not be drinking and is endorsed by the American Medical Association, the National Safety Council, and the American Association of Poison Control Centers. The entire screening and testing procedure shall be explained to the test subject prior to the conduct of the screening test.

(a) Taste Threshold Screening.

The Bitrex taste threshold screening, performed without wearing a respirator, is intended to determine whether the individual being tested can detect the taste of Bitrex.

(1) During threshold screening as well as during fit testing, subjects shall wear an enclosure about the head and shoulders that is approximately 12 inches (30.5 cm) in diameter by 14 inches (35.6 cm) tall. The front portion of the enclosure shall be clear from the respirator and allow free movement of the head when a respirator is worn. An enclosure substantially similar

to the 3M hood assembly, parts # FT 14 and # FT 15 combined, is adequate.

(2) The test enclosure shall have a 3/4 inch (1.9 cm) hole in front of the test subject's nose and mouth area to accommodate the nebulizer nozzle.

(3) The test subject shall don the test enclosure. Throughout the threshold screening test, the test subject shall breathe through his or her slightly open mouth with tongue extended. The subject is instructed to report when he/she detects a bitter taste

(4) Using a DeVilbiss Model 40 Inhalation Medication Nebulizer or equivalent, the test conductor shall spray the Threshold Check Solution into the enclosure. This Nebulizer shall be clearly marked to distinguish it from the fit test solution nebulizer.

(5) The Threshold Check Solution is prepared by adding 13.5 milligrams of Bitrex to 100 ml of 5% salt (NaCl) solution in distilled water.

(6) To produce the aerosol, the nebulizer bulb is firmly squeezed so that the bulb collapses completely, and is then released and allowed to fully expand.

(7) An initial ten squeezes are repeated rapidly and then the test subject is asked whether the Bitrex can be tasted. If the test subject reports tasting the bitter taste during the ten squeezes, the screening test is completed. The taste threshold is noted as ten regardless of the number of squeezes actually completed.

(8) If the first response is negative, ten more squeezes are repeated rapidly and the test subject is again asked whether the Bitrex is tasted. If the test subject reports tasting the bitter taste during the second ten squeezes, the screening test is completed. The taste threshold is noted as twenty regardless of the number of squeezes actually completed.

(9) If the second response is negative, ten more squeezes are repeated rapidly and the test subject is again asked whether the Bitrex is tasted. If the test subject reports tasting the bitter taste during the third set of ten squeezes, the screening test is completed. The taste threshold is noted as thirty regardless of the number of squeezes actually completed.

(10) The test conductor will take note of the number of squeezes required to solicit a taste response.

(11) If the Bitrex is not tasted after 30 squeezes (step 10), the test subject is unable to taste Bitrex and may not perform the Bitrex fit test.

(12) If a taste response is elicited, the test subject shall be asked to take note of the taste for reference in the fit test.

(13) Correct use of the nebulizer means that approximately 1 ml of liquid is used at a time in the nebulizer body.

(14) The nebulizer shall be thoroughly rinsed in water, shaken to dry, and refilled at least each morning and afternoon or at least every four hours.

(b) Bitrex Solution Aerosol Fit Test Procedure.

(1) The test subject may not eat, drink (except plain water), smoke, or chew gum for 15 minutes before the test.

(2) The fit test uses the same enclosure as that described in 4. (a) above.

(3) The test subject shall don the enclosure while wearing the respirator selected according to section I. A. of this appendix. The respirator shall be properly adjusted and equipped with any type particulate filter(s).

(4) A second DeVilbiss Model 40 Inhalation Medication Nebulizer or equivalent is used to spray the fit test solution into the enclosure. This nebulizer shall be clearly marked to distinguish it from the screening test solution nebulizer.

(5) The fit test solution is prepared by adding 337.5 mg of Bitrex to 200 ml of a 5% salt (NaCl) solution in warm water.

(6) As before, the test subject shall breathe through his or her slightly open mouth with tongue extended, and be instructed to report if he/she tastes the bitter taste of Bitrex.

(7) The nebulizer is inserted into the hole in the front of the enclosure and an initial concentration of the fit test solution is sprayed into the enclosure using the same number of squeezes (either 10, 20 or 30 squeezes) based on the num-

ber of squeezes required to elicit a taste response as noted during the screening test.

(8) After generating the aerosol, the test subject shall be instructed to perform the exercises in section I. A. 14. of this appendix.

(9) Every 30 seconds the aerosol concentration shall be replenished using one half the number of squeezes used initially (e.g., 5, 10 or 15).

(10) The test subject shall indicate to the test conductor if at any time during the fit test the taste of Bitrex is detected. If the test subject does not report tasting the Bitrex, the test is passed.

(11) If the taste of Bitrex is detected, the fit is deemed unsatisfactory and the test is failed. A different respirator shall be tried and the entire test procedure is repeated (taste threshold screening and fit testing).

5. Irritant Smoke (Stannic Chloride) Protocol

This qualitative fit test uses a person's response to the irritating chemicals released in the "smoke" produced by a stannic chloride ventilation smoke tube to detect leakage into the respirator.

(a) General Requirements and Precautions

(1) The respirator to be tested shall be equipped with high efficiency particulate air (HEPA) or P100 series filter(s).

(2) Only stannic chloride smoke tubes shall be used for this protocol.

(3) No form of test enclosure or hood for the test subject shall be used.

(4) The smoke can be irritating to the eyes, lungs, and nasal passages. The test conductor shall take precautions to minimize the test subject's exposure to irritant smoke. Sensitivity varies, and certain individuals may respond to a greater degree to irritant smoke. Care shall be taken when performing the sensitivity screening checks that determine whether the test subject can detect irritant smoke to use only the minimum amount of smoke necessary to elicit a response from the test subject.

(5) The fit test shall be performed in an area with adequate ventilation to prevent exposure of the person conducting the fit test or the build-up of irritant smoke in the general atmosphere.

(b) Sensitivity Screening Check

The person to be tested must demonstrate his or her ability to detect a weak concentration of the irritant smoke.

(1) The test operator shall break both ends of a ventilation smoke tube containing stannic chloride, and attach one end of the smoke tube to a low flow air pump set to deliver 200 milliliters per minute, or an aspirator squeeze bulb. The test operator shall cover the other end of the smoke tube with a short piece of tubing to prevent potential injury from the jagged end of the smoke tube.

(2) The test operator shall advise the test subject that the smoke can be irritating to the eyes, lungs, and nasal passages and instruct the subject to keep his/her eyes closed while the test is performed.

(3) The test subject shall be allowed to smell a weak concentration of the irritant smoke before the respirator is donned to become familiar with its irritating properties and to determine if he/she can detect the irritating properties of the smoke. The test operator shall carefully direct a small amount of the irritant smoke in the test subject's direction to determine that he/she can detect it.

(c) Irritant Smoke Fit Test Procedure

(1) The person being fit tested shall don the respirator without assistance, and perform the required user seal check(s).

(2) The test subject shall be instructed to keep his/her eyes closed.

(3) The test operator shall direct the stream of irritant smoke from the smoke tube toward the faceseal area of the test subject, using the low flow pump or the squeeze bulb. The test operator shall begin at least 12 inches from the facepiece and move the smoke stream around the whole perimeter of the mask. The operator shall gradually make two more passes around the perimeter of the mask, moving to within six inches of the respirator.

(4) If the person being tested has not had an involuntary response and/or detected the irritant smoke, proceed with the test exercises.

(5) The exercises identified in section I.A. 14. of this appendix shall be performed by the test subject while the respirator seal is being continually challenged by the smoke, directed around the perimeter of the respirator at a distance of six inches.

(6) If the person being fit tested reports detecting the irritant smoke at any time, the test is failed. The person being retested must repeat the entire sensitivity check and fit test procedure.

(7) Each test subject passing the irritant smoke test without evidence of a response (involuntary cough, irritation) shall be given a second sensitivity screening check, with the smoke from the same smoke tube used during the fit test, once the respirator has been removed, to determine whether he/she still reacts to the smoke. Failure to evoke a response shall void the fit test.

(8) If a response is produced during this second sensitivity check, then the fit test is passed.

C. Quantitative Fit Test (QNFT) Protocols

The following quantitative fit testing procedures have been demonstrated to be acceptable: Quantitative fit testing using a non-hazardous test aerosol (such as corn oil, polyethylene glycol 400 [PEG 400], di-2-ethyl hexyl sebacate [DEHS], or sodium chloride) generated in a test chamber, and employing instrumentation to quantify the fit of the respirator; Quantitative fit testing using ambient aerosol as the test agent and appropriate instrumentation (condensation nuclei counter) to quantify the respirator fit; Quantitative fit testing using controlled negative pressure and appropriate instrumentation to measure the volumetric leak rate of a facepiece to quantify the respirator fit.

1. General

(a) The employer shall ensure that persons administering QNFT are able to calibrate equipment and perform tests properly, recognize invalid tests, calculate fit factors properly and ensure that test equipment is in proper working order.

(b) The employer shall ensure that QNFT equipment is kept clean, and is maintained and calibrated according to the manufacturer's instructions so as to operate at the parameters for which it was designed.

2. Generated Aerosol Quantitative Fit Testing Protocol

(a) Apparatus.

(1) Instrumentation. Aerosol generation, dilution, and measurement systems using particulates (corn oil, polyethylene glycol 400 [PEG 400], di-2-ethyl hexyl sebacate [DEHS] or sodium chloride) as test aerosols shall be used for quantitative fit testing.

(2) Test chamber. The test chamber shall be large enough to permit all test subjects to perform freely all required exercises without disturbing the test agent concentration or the measurement apparatus. The test chamber shall be equipped and constructed so that the test agent is effectively isolated from the ambient air, yet uniform in concentration throughout the chamber.

(3) When testing air-purifying respirators, the normal filter or cartridge element shall be replaced with a high efficiency particulate air (HEPA) or P100 series filter supplied by the same manufacturer.

(4) The sampling instrument shall be selected so that a computer record or strip chart record may be made of the test showing the rise and fall of the test agent concentration with each inspiration and expiration at fit factors of at least 2,000. Integrators or computers that integrate the amount of test agent penetration leakage into the respirator for each exercise may be used provided a record of the readings is made.

(5) The combination of substitute air-purifying elements, test agent and test agent concentration shall be such that the test subject is not exposed in excess of an established exposure limit for the test agent at any time during the testing process, based upon the length of the exposure and the exposure limit duration.

(6) The sampling port on the test specimen respirator shall be placed and constructed so that no leakage occurs around the port (e.g., where the respirator is probed), a free air flow is allowed into the sampling line at all times, and there is no interference with the fit or performance of the respirator. The in-mask sampling device (probe) shall be designed and used so that the air sample is drawn from the breathing zone of the test subject, midway between the nose and mouth and with the probe extending into the facepiece cavity at least 1/4 inch.

(7) The test setup shall permit the person administering the test to observe the test subject inside the chamber during the test.

(8) The equipment generating the test atmosphere shall maintain the concentration of test agent constant to within a 10 percent variation for the duration of the test.

(9) The time lag (interval between an event and the recording of the event on the strip chart or computer or integrator) shall be kept to a minimum. There shall be a clear association between the occurrence of an event and its being recorded.

(10) The sampling line tubing for the test chamber atmosphere and for the respirator sampling port shall be of equal diameter and of the same material. The length of the two lines shall be equal.

(11) The exhaust flow from the test chamber shall pass through an appropriate filter (i.e., high efficiency particulate filter) before release.

(12) When sodium chloride aerosol is used, the relative humidity inside the test chamber shall not exceed 50 percent.

(13) The limitations of instrument detection shall be taken into account when determining the fit factor.

(14) Test respirators shall be maintained in proper working order and be inspected regularly for deficiencies such as cracks or missing valves and gaskets.

(b) Procedural Requirements.

(1) When performing the initial user seal check using a positive or negative pressure check, the sampling line shall be crimped closed in order to avoid air pressure leakage during either of these pressure checks.

(2) The use of an abbreviated screening QLFT test is optional. Such a test may be utilized in order to quickly identify poor fitting respirators that passed the positive and/or negative pressure test and reduce the amount of QNFT time. The use of the CNC QNFT instrument in the count mode is another optional method to obtain a quick estimate of fit and eliminate poor fitting respirators before going on to perform a full QNFT.

(3) A reasonably stable test agent concentration shall be measured in the test chamber prior to testing. For canopy or shower curtain types of test units, the determination of the test agent's stability may be established after the test subject has entered the test environment.

(4) Immediately after the subject enters the test chamber, the test agent concentration inside the respirator shall be measured to ensure that the peak penetration does not exceed 5 percent for a half mask or 1 percent for a full facepiece respirator.

(5) A stable test agent concentration shall be obtained prior to the actual start of testing.

(6) Respirator restraining straps shall not be over-tightened for testing. The straps shall be adjusted by the wearer without assistance from other persons to give a reasonably comfortable fit typical of normal use. The respirator shall not be adjusted once the fit test exercises begin.

(7) The test shall be terminated whenever any single peak penetration exceeds 5 percent for half masks and 1 percent for full facepiece respirators. The test subject shall be refitted and retested.

(8) Calculation of fit factors.

(i) The fit factor shall be determined for the quantitative fit test by taking the ratio of the average chamber concentration to the concentration measured inside the respirator for each test exercise except the grimace exercise.

(ii) The average test chamber concentration shall be calculated as the arithmetic average of the concentration measured before and after each test (i.e., 7 exercises) or the arithmetic average of the concentration measured before and after each exercise or the true average measured continuously during the respirator sample.

(iii) The concentration of the challenge agent inside the respirator shall be determined by one of the following methods:

(A) Average peak penetration method means the method of determining test agent penetration into the respirator utilizing a strip chart recorder, integrator, or computer. The agent penetration is determined by an average of the peak heights on the graph or by computer integration, for each exercise except the grimace exercise. Integrators or computers that calculate the actual test agent penetration into the respirator for each exercise will also be considered to meet the requirements of the average peak penetration method.

(B) Maximum peak penetration method means the method of determining test agent penetration in the respirator as determined by strip chart recordings of the test. The highest peak penetration for a given exercise is taken to be representative of average penetration into the respirator for that exercise.

(C) Integration by calculation of the area under the individual peak for each exercise except the grimace exercise. This includes computerized integration.

(D) The calculation of the overall fit factor using individual exercise fit factors involves first converting the exercise fit factors to penetration values, determining the average, and then converting that result back to a fit factor. This procedure is described in the following equation:

$$\text{Overall Fit Factor} = \frac{\text{Number of exercises}}{1/ff_1 + 1/ff_2 + 1/ff_3 + 1/ff_4 + 1/ff_5 + 1/ff_6 + 1/ff_7 + 1/ff_8}$$

Where ff_1, ff_2, ff_3, etc. are the fit factors for exercises 1, 2, 3, etc.

(9) The test subject shall not be permitted to wear a half mask or quarter facepiece respirator unless a minimum fit factor of 100 is obtained, or a full facepiece respirator unless a minimum fit factor of 500 is obtained.

(10) Filters used for quantitative fit testing shall be replaced whenever increased breathing resistance is encountered, or when the test agent has altered the integrity of the filter media.

3. Ambient aerosol condensation nuclei counter (CNC) quantitative fit testing protocol.

The ambient aerosol condensation nuclei counter (CNC) quantitative fit testing (Portacount ™) protocol quantitatively fit tests respirators with the use of a probe. The probed respirator is only used for quantitative fit tests. A probed respirator has a special sampling device, installed on the respirator, that allows the probe to sample the air from inside the mask. A probed respirator is required for each make, style, model, and size that the employer uses and can be obtained from the respirator manufacturer or distributor. The CNC instrument manufacturer, TSI Inc., also provides probe attachments (TSI sampling adapters) that permit fit testing in an employee's own respirator. A minimum fit factor pass level of at least 100 is necessary for a half-mask respirator and a minimum fit factor pass level of at least 500 is required for a full facepiece negative pressure respirator. The entire screening and testing procedure shall be explained to the test subject prior to the conduct of the screening test.

(a) Portacount Fit Test Requirements.

(1) Check the respirator to make sure the sampling probe and line are properly attached to the facepiece and that the respirator is fitted with a particulate filter capable of preventing significant penetration by the ambient particles used for the fit test (e.g., NIOSH 42 CFR 84 series 100, series 99, or series 95 particulate filter) per manufacturer's instruction.

(2) Instruct the person to be tested to don the respirator for five minutes before the fit test starts. This purges the ambient particles trapped inside the respirator and permits the wearer to make certain the respirator is comfortable. This individual shall already have been trained on how to wear the respirator properly.

(3) Check the following conditions for the adequacy of the respirator fit: Chin properly placed; Adequate strap tension, not overly tightened; Fit across nose bridge; Respirator of proper size to span distance from nose to chin; Tendency of the respirator to slip; Self-observation in a mirror to evaluate fit and respirator position.

(4) Have the person wearing the respirator do a user seal check. If leakage is detected, determine the cause. If leakage is from a poorly fitting facepiece, try another size of the same model respirator, or another model of respirator.

(5) Follow the manufacturer's instructions for operating the Portacount and proceed with the test.

(6) The test subject shall be instructed to perform the exercises in section I. A. 14. of this appendix.

(7) After the test exercises, the test subject shall be questioned by the test conductor regarding

the comfort of the respirator upon completion of the protocol. If it has become unacceptable, another model of respirator shall be tried.

(b) Portacount Test Instrument.

(1) The Portacount will automatically stop and calculate the overall fit factor for the entire set of exercises. The overall fit factor is what counts. The Pass or Fail message will indicate whether or not the test was successful. If the test was a Pass, the fit test is over.

(2) Since the pass or fail criterion of the Portacount is user programmable, the test operator shall ensure that the pass or fail criterion meet the requirements for minimum respirator performance in this Appendix.

(3) A record of the test needs to be kept on file, assuming the fit test was successful. The record must contain the test subject's name; overall fit factor; make, model, style, and size of respirator used; and date tested.

4. Controlled negative pressure (CNP) quantitative fit testing protocol.

The CNP protocol provides an alternative to aerosol fit test methods. The CNP fit test method technology is based on exhausting air from a temporarily sealed respirator facepiece to generate and then maintain a constant negative pressure inside the facepiece. The rate of air exhaust is controlled so that a constant negative pressure is maintained in the respirator during the fit test. The level of pressure is selected to replicate the mean inspiratory pressure that causes leakage into the respirator under normal use conditions. With pressure held constant, air flow out of the respirator is equal to air flow into the respirator. Therefore, measurement of the exhaust stream that is required to hold the pressure in the temporarily sealed respirator constant yields a direct measure of leakage air flow into the respirator. The CNP fit test method measures leak rates through the facepiece as a method for determining the facepiece fit for negative pressure respirators. The CNP instrument manufacturer Occupational Health Dynamics of Birmingham, Alabama also provides attachments (sampling manifolds) that replace the filter cartridges to permit fit testing in an employee's own respirator. To perform the test, the test subject closes his or her mouth and holds his/her breath, after which an air pump removes air from the respirator facepiece at a pre-selected constant pressure. The facepiece fit is expressed as the leak rate through the facepiece, expressed as milliliters per minute. The quality and va-

lidity of the CNP fit tests are determined by the degree to which the in-mask pressure tracks the test pressure during the system measurement time of approximately five seconds. Instantaneous feedback in the form of a real-time pressure trace of the in-mask pressure is provided and used to determine test validity and quality. A minimum fit factor pass level of 100 is necessary for a half-mask respirator and a minimum fit factor of at least 500 is required for a full facepiece respirator. The entire screening and testing procedure shall be explained to the test subject prior to the conduct of the screening test.

(a) CNP Fit Test Requirements.

(1) The instrument shall have a non-adjustable test pressure of 15.0 mm water pressure.

(2) The CNP system defaults selected for test pressure shall be set at -- 15 mm of water (-0.58 inches of water) and the modeled inspiratory flow rate shall be 53.8 liters per minute for performing fit tests.

(**Note:** CNP systems have built-in capability to conduct fit testing that is specific to unique work rate, mask, and gender situations that might apply in a specific workplace. Use of system default values, which were selected to represent respirator wear with medium cartridge resistance at a low-moderate work rate, will allow inter-test comparison of the respirator fit.)

(3) The individual who conducts the CNP fit testing shall be thoroughly trained to perform the test.

(4) The respirator filter or cartridge needs to be replaced with the CNP test manifold. The inhalation valve downstream from the manifold either needs to be temporarily removed or propped open.

(5) The employer must train the test subject to hold his or her breath for at least 10 seconds.

(6) The test subject must don the test respirator without any assistance from the test administrator who is conducting the CNP fit test. The respirator must not be adjusted once the fit-test exercises begin. Any adjustment voids the test, and the test subject must repeat the fit test.

(7) The QNFT protocol shall be followed according to section I. C. 1. of this appendix with an exception for the CNP test exercises.

(b) CNP Test Exercises.

(1) Normal breathing. In a normal standing position, without talking, the subject shall breathe normally for 1 minute. After the normal breathing exercise, the subject needs to hold head straight ahead and hold his or her breath for 10 seconds during the test measurement.

(2) Deep breathing. In a normal standing position, the subject shall breathe slowly and deeply for 1 minute, being careful not to hyperventilate. After the deep breathing exercise, the subject shall hold his or her head straight ahead and hold his or her breath for 10 seconds during test measurement.

(3) Turning head side to side. Standing in place, the subject shall slowly turn his or her head from side to side between the extreme positions on each side for 1 minute. The head shall be held at each extreme momentarily so the subject can inhale at each side. After the turning head side to side exercise, the subject needs to hold head full left and hold his or her breath for 10 seconds during test measurement. Next, the subject needs to hold head full right and hold his or her breath for 10 seconds during test measurement.

(4) Moving head up and down. Standing in place, the subject shall slowly move his or her head up and down for 1 minute. The subject shall be instructed to inhale in the up position (i.e., when looking toward the ceiling). After the moving head up and down exercise, the subject shall hold his or her head full up and hold his or her breath for 10 seconds during test measurement. Next, the subject shall hold his or her head full down and hold his or her breath for 10 seconds during test measurement.

(5) Talking. The subject shall talk out loud slowly and loud enough so as to be heard clearly by the test conductor. The subject can read from a prepared text such as the Rainbow Passage, count backward from 100, or recite a memorized poem or song for 1 minute. After the talking exercise, the subject shall hold his or her head straight ahead and hold his or her breath for 10 seconds during the test measurement.

(6) Grimace. The test subject shall grimace by smiling or frowning for 15 seconds.

(7) Bending Over. The test subject shall bend at the waist as if he or she were to touch his or her toes for 1 minute. Jogging in place shall be sub-

stituted for this exercise in those test environments such as shroud-type QNFT units that prohibit bending at the waist. After the bending over exercise, the subject shall hold his or her head straight ahead and hold his or her breath for 10 seconds during the test measurement.

(8) Normal Breathing. The test subject shall remove and re-don the respirator within a one-minute period. Then, in a normal standing position, without talking, the subject shall breathe normally for 1 minute. After the normal breathing exercise, the subject shall hold his or her head straight ahead and hold his or her breath for 10 seconds during the test measurement. After the test exercises, the test subject shall be questioned by the test conductor regarding the comfort of the respirator upon completion of the protocol. If it has become unacceptable, another model of a respirator shall be tried.

(c) CNP Test Instrument.

(1) The test instrument must have an effective audio-warning device, or a visual-warning device in the form of a screen tracing, that indicates when the test subject fails to hold his or her breath during the test. The test must be terminated and restarted from the beginning when the test subject fails to hold his or her breath during the test. The test subject then may be refitted and retested.

(2) A record of the test shall be kept on file, assuming the fit test was successful. The record must contain the test subject's name; overall fit factor; make, model, style and size of respirator used; and date tested.

5. Controlled negative pressure (CNP) REDON quantitative fit testing protocol.

(a) When administering this protocol to test subjects, employers must comply with the requirements specified in paragraphs (a) and (c) of Part I.C.4 of this appendix ("Controlled negative pressure (CNP) quantitative fit testing protocol"), as well as use the test exercises described below in paragraph (b) of this protocol instead of the test exercises specified in paragraph (b) of Part I.C.4 of this appendix.

(b) Employers must ensure that each test subject being fit tested using this protocol follows the exercise and measurement procedures, including the order of administration, described below in Table A-1 of this appendix.

Table A-1. CNP REDON Quantitative Fit Testing Protocol

Exercises(1)	Exercise procedure	Measurement procedure
Facing Forward	Stand and breathe normally, without talking, for 30 seconds.	Face forward, while holding breath for 10 seconds.
Bending Over	Bend at the waist, as if going to touch his or her toes, for 30 seconds.	Face parallel to the floor, while holding breath for 10 seconds
Head Shaking	For about three seconds, shake head back and forth vigorously several times while shouting.	Face forward, while holding breath for 10 seconds.
REDON 1	Remove the respirator mask, loosen all facepiece straps, and then redon the respirator mask.	Face forward, while holding breath for 10 seconds.
REDON 2	Remove the respirator mask, loosen all facepiece straps, and then redon the respirator mask again.	Face forward, while holding breath for 10 seconds.

[1] Exercises are listed in the order in which they are to be administered.

(c) After completing the test exercises, the test administrator must question each test subject regarding the comfort of the respirator. When a test subject states that the respirator is unacceptable, the employer must ensure that the test administrator repeats the protocol using another respirator model.

(d) Employers must determine the overall fit factor for each test subject by calculating the harmonic mean of the fit testing exercises as follows:

$$\text{Overall Fit Factor} = \frac{N}{[1/FF_1 + 1/FF_2 + \ldots 1/FF_N]}$$

Where:
N = The number of exercises;
FF_1 = The fit factor for the first exercise;
FF_2 = The fit factor for the second exercise; and
FF_N = The fit factor for the nth exercise.

Part II. New Fit Test Protocols

A. Any person may submit to OSHA an application for approval of a new fit test protocol. If the application meets the following criteria, OSHA will initiate a rulemaking proceeding under section 6(b)(7) of the OSH Act to determine whether to list the new protocol as an approved protocol in this Appendix A.

B. The application must include a detailed description of the proposed new fit test protocol. This application must be supported by either:

1. A test report prepared by an independent government research laboratory (e.g., Lawrence Livermore National Laboratory, Los Alamos National Laboratory, the National Institute for Standards and Technology) stating that the laboratory has tested the protocol and had found it to be accurate and reliable; or

2. An article that has been published in a peer-reviewed industrial hygiene journal describing the protocol and explaining how test data support the protocol's accuracy and reliability.

C. If OSHA determines that additional information is required before the Agency commences a rulemaking proceeding under this section, OSHA will so notify the applicant and afford the applicant the opportunity to submit the supplemental information. Initiation of a rulemaking proceeding will be deferred until OSHA has received and evaluated the supplemental information.

Appendix B-1 to §1910.134: User Seal Check Procedures (Mandatory)

The individual who uses a tight-fitting respirator is to perform a user seal check to ensure that an adequate seal is achieved each time the respirator is put on. Either the positive and negative pressure checks listed in this appendix, or the respirator manufacturer's recommended user seal check method shall be used. User seal checks are not substitutes for qualitative or quantitative fit tests.

I. Facepiece Positive and/or Negative Pressure Checks

A. Positive pressure check. Close off the exhalation valve and exhale gently into the facepiece. The face fit is considered satisfactory if a slight positive pressure can be built up inside the facepiece without any evidence of outward leakage of air at the seal. For most respirators this method of leak testing requires the wearer to first remove the exhalation valve cover before closing off the exhalation valve and then carefully replacing it after the test.

B. Negative pressure check. Close off the inlet opening of the canister or cartridge(s) by covering with the palm of the hand(s) or by replacing the filter seal(s), inhale gently so that the facepiece collapses slightly, and hold the breath for ten seconds. The design of the inlet opening of some cartridges cannot be effectively covered with the palm of the hand. The test can be performed by covering the inlet opening of the cartridge with a thin latex or nitrile glove. If the facepiece remains in its slightly collapsed condition and no inward leakage of air is detected, the tightness of the respirator is considered satisfactory.

II. Manufacturer's Recommended User Seal Check Procedures

The respirator manufacturer's recommended procedures for performing a user seal check may be used instead of the positive and/or negative pressure check procedures provided that the employer demonstrates that the manufacturer's procedures are equally effective.

Appendix B-2 to §1910.134: Respirator Cleaning Procedures (Mandatory)

These procedures are provided for employer use when cleaning respirators. They are general in nature, and the employer as an alternative may use the cleaning recommendations provided by the manufacturer of the respirators used by their employees, provided such procedures are as effective as those listed here in Appendix B- 2. Equivalent effectiveness simply means that the procedures used must accomplish the objectives set forth in Appendix B-2, i.e., must ensure that the respirator is properly cleaned and disinfected in a manner that prevents damage to the respirator and does not cause harm to the user.

I. Procedures for Cleaning Respirators

A. Remove filters, cartridges, or canisters. Disassemble facepieces by removing speaking diaphragms, demand and pressure-demand valve assemblies, hoses, or any components recommended by the manufacturer. Discard or repair any defective parts.

B. Wash components in warm (43 deg. C [110 deg. F] maximum) water with a mild detergent or with a cleaner recommended by the manufacturer. A stiff bristle (not wire) brush may be used to facilitate the removal of dirt.

C. Rinse components thoroughly in clean, warm (43 deg. C [110 deg. F] maximum), preferably running water. Drain.

D. When the cleaner used does not contain a disinfecting agent, respirator components should be immersed for two minutes in one of the following:

1. Hypochlorite solution (50 ppm of chlorine) made by adding approximately one milliliter of laundry bleach to one liter of water at 43 deg. C (110 deg. F); or,

2. Aqueous solution of iodine (50 ppm iodine) made by adding approximately 0.8 milliliters of tincture of iodine (6-8 grams ammonium and/or potassium iodide/100 cc of 45% alcohol) to one liter of water at 43 deg. C (110 deg. F); or,

3. Other commercially available cleansers of equivalent disinfectant quality when used as directed, if their use is recommended or approved by the respirator manufacturer.

E. Rinse components thoroughly in clean, warm (43 deg. C [110 deg. F] maximum), preferably running water. Drain. The importance of thorough rinsing cannot be overemphasized. Detergents or disinfectants that dry on facepieces may result in dermatitis. In addition, some disinfectants may cause deterioration of rubber or corrosion of metal parts if not completely removed.

F. Components should be hand-dried with a clean lint-free cloth or air-dried.

G. Reassemble facepiece, replacing filters, cartridges, and canisters where necessary.

H. Test the respirator to ensure that all components work properly.

Appendix C to §1910.134: OSHA Respirator Medical Evaluation Questionnaire (Mandatory)

To the employer: Answers to questions in Section 1, and to question 9 in Section 2 of Part A, do not require a medical examination.

To the employee:

Can you read (circle one): Yes/No

Your employer must allow you to answer this questionnaire during normal working hours, or at a time and place that is convenient to you. To maintain your confidentiality, your employer or supervisor must not look at or review your answers, and your employer must tell you how to deliver or send this questionnaire to the health care professional who will review it.

Part A. Section 1. (Mandatory)

The following information must be provided by every employee who has been selected to use any type of respirator (please print).

1. Today's date:_____

2. Your name:_____

3. Your age (to nearest year):_____

4. Sex (circle one): Male/Female

5. Your height: _____ ft. _____ in.

6. Your weight: _____ lbs.

7. Your job title:_____

8. A phone number where you can be reached by the health care professional who reviews this questionnaire (include the Area Code): _____

9. The best time to phone you at this number:

_____

10. Has your employer told you how to contact the health care professional who will review this questionnaire (circle one): Yes/No

11. Check the type of respirator you will use (you can check more than one category):

a. _____ N, R, or P disposable respirator (filter-mask, non-cartridge type only).

b. _____ Other type (for example, half- or full-face-piece type, powered-air purifying, supplied-air, self-contained breathing apparatus).

12. Have you worn a respirator (circle one): Yes/No

If "yes," what type(s):_____
_____
_____

Part A. Section 2. (Mandatory)

Questions 1 through 9 below must be answered by every employee who has been selected to use any type of respirator (please circle "yes" or "no").

1. Do you **currently** smoke tobacco, or have you smoked tobacco in the last month: Yes/No

2. Have you **ever had** any of the following conditions?

Seizures (fits): Yes/No

Diabetes (sugar disease): Yes/No

Allergic reactions that interfere with your breathing: Yes/No

Claustrophobia (fear of closed-in places): Yes/No

Trouble smelling odors: Yes/No

3. Have you **ever had** any of the following pulmonary or lung problems?

Asbestosis: Yes/No

Asthma: Yes/No

Chronic bronchitis: Yes/No

Emphysema: Yes/No

Pneumonia: Yes/No

Tuberculosis: Yes/No

Silicosis: Yes/No

Pneumothorax (collapsed lung): Yes/No

Lung cancer: Yes/No

Broken ribs: Yes/No

Any chest injuries or surgeries: Yes/No

Any other lung problem that you've been told about: Yes/No

4. Do you **currently** have any of the following symptoms of pulmonary or lung illness?

OSHA®
Occupational Safety and
Health Administration

Shortness of breath: Yes/No

Shortness of breath when walking fast on level ground or walking up a slight hill or incline: Yes/No

Shortness of breath when walking with other people at an ordinary pace on level ground: Yes/No

Have to stop for breath when walking at your own pace on level ground: Yes/No

Shortness of breath when washing or dressing yourself: Yes/No

Shortness of breath that interferes with your job: Yes/No

Coughing that produces phlegm (thick sputum): Yes/No

Coughing that wakes you early in the morning: Yes/No

Coughing that occurs mostly when you are lying down: Yes/No

Coughing up blood in the last month: Yes/No

Wheezing: Yes/No

Wheezing that interferes with your job: Yes/No

Chest pain when you breathe deeply: Yes/No

Any other symptoms that you think may be related to lung problems: Yes/No

5. Have you **ever had** any of the following cardiovascular or heart problems?

Heart attack: Yes/No

Stroke: Yes/No

Angina: Yes/No

Heart failure: Yes/No

Swelling in your legs or feet (not caused by walking): Yes/No

Heart arrhythmia (heart beating irregularly): Yes/No

High blood pressure: Yes/No

Any other heart problem that you've been told about: Yes/No

6. Have you **ever had** any of the following cardiovascular or heart symptoms?

Frequent pain or tightness in your chest: Yes/No

Pain or tightness in your chest during physical activity: Yes/No

Pain or tightness in your chest that interferes with your job: Yes/No

In the past two years, have you noticed your heart skipping or missing a beat: Yes/No

Heartburn or indigestion that is not related to eating: Yes/ No

Any other symptoms that you think may be related to heart or circulation problems: Yes/No

7. Do you **currently** take medication for any of the following problems?

Breathing or lung problems: Yes/No

Heart trouble: Yes/No

Blood pressure: Yes/No

Seizures (fits): Yes/No

8. If you've used a respirator, have you **ever had** any of the following problems? (If you've never used a respirator, check the following space and go to question 9:)

Eye irritation: Yes/No

Skin allergies or rashes: Yes/No

Anxiety: Yes/No

General weakness or fatigue: Yes/No

Any other problem that interferes with your use of a respirator: Yes/No

9. Would you like to talk to the health care professional who will review this questionnaire about your answers to this questionnaire: Yes/No

Questions 10 to 15 below must be answered by every employee who has been selected to use either a full-facepiece respirator or a self-contained breathing apparatus (SCBA). For employees who have been selected to use other types of respirators, answering these questions is voluntary.

10. Have you **ever lost** vision in either eye (temporarily or permanently): Yes/No

11. Do you **currently** have any of the following vision problems?

Wear contact lenses: Yes/No

Wear glasses: Yes/No

Color blind: Yes/No

Any other eye or vision problem: Yes/No

12. Have you **ever had** an injury to your ears, including a broken ear drum: Yes/No

13. Do you **currently** have any of the following hearing problems?

Difficulty hearing: Yes/No

Wear a hearing aid: Yes/No

Any other hearing or ear problem: Yes/No

14. Have you **ever had** a back injury: Yes/No

15. Do you **currently** have any of the following musculoskeletal problems?

Weakness in any of your arms, hands, legs, or feet: Yes/No

Back pain: Yes/No

Difficulty fully moving your arms and legs: Yes/No

Pain or stiffness when you lean forward or backward at the waist: Yes/No

Difficulty fully moving your head up or down: Yes/No

Difficulty fully moving your head side to side: Yes/No

Difficulty bending at your knees: Yes/No

Difficulty squatting to the ground: Yes/No

Climbing a flight of stairs or a ladder carrying more than 25 lbs: Yes/No

Any other muscle or skeletal problem that interferes with using a respirator: Yes/No

Part B

Any of the following questions, and other questions not listed, may be added to the questionnaire at the discretion of the health care professional who will review the questionnaire.

1. In your present job, are you working at high altitudes (over 5,000 feet) or in a place that has lower than normal amounts of oxygen: Yes/No

    If "yes," do you have feelings of dizziness, shortness of breath, pounding in your chest, or other symptoms when you're working under these conditions: Yes/No

2. At work or at home, have you ever been exposed to hazardous solvents, hazardous airborne chemicals (e.g., gases, fumes, or dust), or have you come into skin contact with hazardous chemicals: Yes/No

    If "yes," name the chemicals if you know them:_____
    _____
    _____
    _____

3. Have you ever worked with any of the materials, or under any of the conditions, listed below:

    Asbestos: Yes/No

    Silica (e.g., in sandblasting): Yes/No

    Tungsten/cobalt (e.g., grinding or welding this material): Yes/No

    Beryllium: Yes/No

    Aluminum: Yes/No

    Coal (for example, mining): Yes/No

    Iron: Yes/No

    Tin: Yes/No

    Dusty environments: Yes/No

    Any other hazardous exposures: Yes/No

If "yes," describe these exposures:_____
_____
_____
_____

4. List any second jobs or side businesses you have:_____
_____

5. List your previous occupations:_____
_____
_____

6. List your current and previous hobbies:_____
_____
_____

7. Have you been in the military services? Yes/No

    If "yes," were you exposed to biological or chemical agents (either in training or combat): Yes/No

8. Have you ever worked on a HAZMAT team? Yes/No

9. Other than medications for breathing and lung problems, heart trouble, blood pressure, and seizures mentioned earlier in this questionnaire, are you taking any other medications for any reason (including over-the-counter medications): Yes/No

    If "yes," name the medications if you know them:_____

10. Will you be using any of the following items with your respirator(s)?
    HEPA Filters: Yes/No
    Canisters (for example, gas masks): Yes/No
    Cartridges: Yes/No

11. How often are you expected to use the respirator(s) (circle "yes" or "no" for all answers that apply to you)?:

    Escape only (no rescue): Yes/No

    Emergency rescue only: Yes/No

    Less than 5 hours **per week**: Yes/No

    Less than 2 hours **per day**: Yes/No

    2 to 4 hours per day: Yes/No

    Over 4 hours per day: Yes/No

12. During the period you are using the respirator(s), is your work effort:

    Light (less than 200 kcal per hour): Yes/No

    If "yes," how long does this period last during the average shift:_____hrs._____mins.

    Examples of a light work effort are **sitting** while

Occupational Safety and Health Administration

writing, typing, drafting, or performing light assembly work; or **standing** while operating a drill press (1-3 lbs.) or controlling machines.

Moderate (200 to 350 kcal per hour): Yes/No

If "yes," how long does this period last during the average shift:_____hrs._____mins.

Examples of moderate work effort are **sitting** while nailing or filing; **driving** a truck or bus in urban traffic; standing while drilling, nailing, performing assembly work, or transferring a moderate load (about 35 lbs.) at trunk level; **walking** on a level surface about 2 mph or down a 5-degree grade about 3 mph; or **pushing** a wheelbarrow with a heavy load (about 100 lbs.) on a level surface.

Heavy (above 350 kcal per hour): Yes/No

If "yes," how long does this period last during the average shift:_____hrs._____mins.

Examples of heavy work are **lifting** a heavy load (about 50 lbs.) from the floor to your waist or shoulder; working on a loading dock; **shoveling**; **standing** while bricklaying or chipping castings; **walking** up an 8-degree grade about 2 mph; climbing stairs with a heavy load (about 50 lbs.).

13. Will you be wearing protective clothing and/or equipment (other than the respirator) when you're using your respirator: Yes/No

If "yes," describe this protective clothing and/or equipment:_____

_____

14. Will you be working under hot conditions (temperature exceeding 77 deg. F): Yes/No

15. Will you be working under humid conditions: Yes/No

16. Describe the work you'll be doing while you're using your respirator(s)_____

_____

_____

17. Describe any special or hazardous conditions you might encounter when you're using your respirator(s) (for example, confined spaces, life-threatening gases):_____

_____

_____

_____

18. Provide the following information, if you know it, for each toxic substance that you'll be exposed to when you're using your respirator(s):

Name of the first toxic substance:_____

_____

Estimated maximum exposure level per shift:_____

Duration of exposure per shift:_____

Name of the second toxic substance:_____

Estimated maximum exposure level per shift:_____

Duration of exposure per shift:_____

Name of the third toxic substance:_____

Estimated maximum exposure level per shift:_____

Duration of exposure per shift:_____

The name of any other toxic substances that you'll be exposed to while using your respirator:

_____

_____

_____

_____

_____

_____

19. Describe any special responsibilities you'll have while using your respirator(s) that may affect the safety and well-being of others (for example, rescue, security):

_____

_____

_____

_____

Appendix D to §1910.134: Information for Employees Using Respirators When Not Required Under the Standard (Mandatory)

Respirators are an effective method of protection against designated hazards when properly selected and worn. Respirator use is encouraged, even when exposures are below the exposure limit, to provide an additional level of comfort and protection for workers. However, if a respirator is used improperly or not kept clean, the respirator itself can become a hazard to the worker. Sometimes, workers may wear respirators to avoid exposures to hazards, even if the amount of hazardous substance does not exceed the limits set by OSHA standards. If your employer provides respirators for your voluntary use, or if you provide your own respirator, you need to take certain precautions to be sure that the respirator itself does not present a hazard.

You should do the following:

1. Read and heed all instructions provided by the manufacturer on use, maintenance, cleaning and care, and warnings regarding the respirators limitations.

2. Choose respirators certified for use to protect against the contaminant of concern. NIOSH, the National Institute for Occupational Safety and Health of the U.S. Department of Health and Human Services, certifies respirators. A label or statement of certification should appear on the respirator or respirator packaging. It will tell you what the respirator is designed for and how much it will protect you.

3. Do not wear your respirator into atmospheres containing contaminants for which your respirator is not designed to protect against. For example, a respirator designed to filter dust particles will not protect you against gases, vapors, or very small solid particles of fumes or smoke.

4. Keep track of your respirator so that you do not mistakenly use someone else's respirator.

[63 FR 1152, Jan. 8, 1998; 63 FR 20098, 20099, April 23, 1998; assembled at 69 FR 46993, Aug. 4, 2004, 71 FR 16672, April 3, 2006; 71 FR 50187, August 24, 2006]

Occupational Safety and Health Administration

Attachment 4:
Sample Program

Small Entity Compliance Guide: Sample Respiratory Protection Program (fill in blanks with your company's/facility's information).

TABLE OF CONTENTS

1. Purpose

_____ has determined that employees in the Prep, Coating, Assembly, and Maintenance departments are exposed to respiratory hazards during routine operations. These hazards include wood dust, particulates, and vapors, and in some cases represent Immediately Dangerous to Life or Health (IDLH) conditions. The purpose of this program is to ensure that all _____ employees are protected from exposure to these respiratory hazards.

Engineering controls, such as ventilation and substitution of less toxic materials, are the first line of defense at _____; however, engineering controls have not always been feasible for some of our operations, or have not always completely controlled the identified hazards. In these situations, respirators and other protective equipment must be used. Respirators are also needed to protect employees' health during emergencies. The work processes requiring respirator use at _____ are outlined in Table 1 in the Scope and Application section of this program.

In addition, some employees have expressed a desire to wear respirators during certain operations that do not require respiratory protection. As a general policy _____ will review each of these requests on a case-by-case basis. If the use of respiratory protection in a specific case will not jeopardize the health or safety of the employee(s), _____ will provide respirators for voluntary use. As outlined in the Scope and Application section of this program, voluntary respirator use is subject to certain requirements of this program.

2. Scope and Application

This program applies to all employees who are required to wear respirators during normal work operations, and during some non-routine or emergency operations such as a spill of a hazardous substance. This includes workers in the Prep, Coating (Spray Booth), Assembly, and Maintenance departments. All employees working in these areas and engaged in certain processes or tasks (as outlined in the table below) must be enrolled in the company's respiratory protection program.

In addition, any employee who voluntarily wears a respirator when a respirator is not required (i.e., in certain maintenance and coating operations) is subject to the medical evaluation, cleaning, maintenance, and storage elements of this program, and must be provided with certain information specified in this section of the program.

Table 1: Voluntary and Required Respirator Use at _____

Type of Respirator	Employee Work Area	Conditions of Use
Filtering facepiece (dust mask)	Warehouse workers	Voluntary
Filtering facepiece	Maintenance workers when cleaning spray booth walls or changing spray booth filter	Voluntary
PAPR with P100 filter	Preparation and Assembly	Mandatory
SAR, pressure demand, with auxiliary SCBA	Maintenance - dip coat tank cleaning	Mandatory
Continuous flow SAR with hood	Spray booth operations (prep and cleaning)	Mandatory
Half facepiece APR, with organic vapor cartridge	Dip Coat Tenders, Spray Maintenance workers and loading coating agents into supply system	Voluntary
Escape SCBA	Dip Coat, Coatings Storage Area, Spray Booth Cleaning Area until ventilation is installed	Mandatory

3. Responsibilities

Program Administrator: the Program Administrator is responsible for administering the respiratory protection program. Duties of the program administrator include:

- Identifying work areas, processes or tasks that require workers to wear respirators, and evaluating hazards.

- Ensuring adequate air quantity, quality, and flow of breathing air for atmosphere-supplying respirators. _(See (c)(1) of the standard.)_

- Selection of respiratory protection options.

- Monitoring respirator use to ensure that respirators are used in accord with their certifications.

- Arranging for and/or conducting training.

- Ensuring proper storage, cleaning, inspections, and maintenance of respiratory protection equipment.

- Conducting qualitative fit testing with Bitrex.

- Administering the medical surveillance program.

- Maintaining records required by the program.

- Evaluating the program.

- Updating written program, as needed.

- The Program Administrator for_____ is _____.

Supervisors: supervisors are responsible for ensuring that the respiratory protection program is implemented in their particular areas. In addition to being knowledgeable about the program requirements for their own protection, supervisors must also ensure that the program is understood and followed by the workers under their charge. _Note: Workers participating in the respiratory protection program do so at no cost to themselves._

Duties of the supervisor include:

- Ensuring that employees under their supervision (including new hires) have received appropriate training, fit testing, and annual medical evaluation.

- Ensuring the availability of appropriate respirators and accessories.

- Being aware of tasks requiring the use of respiratory protection.

- Enforcing the proper use of respiratory protection when necessary.

- Ensuring that respirators are properly cleaned, maintained, inspected, and stored according to the respiratory protection plan.

- Ensuring that respirators fit well and do not cause discomfort.

Occupational Safety and Health Administration

- Continually monitoring work areas and operations to identify respiratory hazards.
- Coordinating with the Program Administrator on how to address respiratory hazards or other concerns regarding the program.
- Ensuring adequate air quantity, quality, and flow of breathing air for atmosphere-supplying respirators. *(See (c)(1) of the standard.)*

Employees: each employee has the responsibility:

- To wear his or her respirator when and where required and in the manner in which they were trained.
- Care for and maintain their respirators as instructed, and store them in a clean, sanitary location.
- Inform their supervisor if the respirator no longer fits well, and request a new one that fits properly.
- Inform their supervisor or the Program Administrator of any respiratory hazards that they feel are not adequately addressed in the workplace and of any other concerns that they have regarding the program.
- Inform their supervisor of need for a medical reevaluation.

4. Program Elements

Selection Procedures – The Program Administrator:

- Will select respirators to be used on site, based on the hazards to which workers are exposed and in accord with all applicable OSHA standards.
- Will conduct a hazard evaluation for each operation, process, or work area where airborne contaminants may be present in routine operations or during an emergency.
- Monitoring can be contracted out.
- The hazard evaluation will include:
  - Identification and development of a list of hazardous substances used in the workplace, by department or work process.
  - Review of work processes to determine where potential exposures to these hazardous substances may occur. This review is to be conducted by surveying the workplace, reviewing process records, and talking with employees and supervisors.
  - Exposure monitoring to quantify potential hazardous exposures.
  - If worker exposures have not been, or cannot be, evaluated they must be considered IDLH.

- Respirators are selected based on the workplace hazards evaluated, and workplace and user factors affecting respirator performance and reliability.
- Respirators are selected based on the Assigned Protection Factors (APFs) and calculated Maximum Use Concentrations (MUCs).
- A sufficient number of respirator sizes and models must be provided to the employee during fit testing to identify the acceptable respirator that correctly fits the users.
- For IDLH atmospheres:
  - Full facepiece pressure demand SARs with auxiliary SCBA unit or full facepiece pressure demand SCBAs, with a minimum service life of 30 minutes, must be provided.
  - Respirators used for escape only are NIOSH-certified for the atmosphere in which they will be used.
  - Oxygen deficient atmospheres are considered IDLH.
- For Non-IDLH atmospheres, respirators are:
  - Selected as appropriate for the APFs and MUCs.
  - Selected as appropriate for the chemical nature and physical form of the contaminant.
  - Equipped with end-of-service-life indicators (ESLIs) if the respirators (APRs) are used for protection against gases and vapors. If there is no ESLI, then a change schedule must be implemented.
  - Equipped with NIOSH-certified HEPA filters (or other filters certified by NIOSH for particulates under 42 CFR part 84) if the respirators (APRs) are to be used for protection against particulates.
- When monitoring is contracted out, an example of the type of statement needed in the respirator program is: _____ currently has a contract with _____ to provide monitoring when needed.

Note: Table 2 at the end of this program contains the sampling data on which this section was based. The results of the current hazard evaluation are the following:

- Prep-sanding: Ventilation controls on some sanders are in place, but employees continue to be exposed to respirable wood dust at 2.5 - 7.0 mg/m^3 (8-hour time-weighted average, or TWA). Half facepiece APRs with P100 filters and goggles are required for employees sanding wood pieces. PAPRs will be available for employees who are unable to wear an APR.

- Prep-cleaning: Average methylene chloride exposures measured at 70 ppm based on 8-hour TWA exposure results for workers cleaning/stripping furniture pieces. Ventilation controls are planned but will not be implemented until designs are completed and a contract has been let for installation of the controls. In the meantime, workers must wear supplied-air hoods with continuous air flow, as required by the Methylene Chloride standard at 29 CFR 1910.1052.

- Coating-spray booth: _____
has decided to take a conservative approach and require all employees to wear supplied-air respirators when working inside the spray booth. Based on exposure data in published reports on the same type of spray booth operations, the **Program Administrator** has determined that a SAR in the continuous flow mode will provide sufficient protection. Spray booth employees may opt to wear half facepiece APRs with organic vapor cartridges when cleaning spray guns.

- Coating-dip coat and drying: Exposures are kept within PELs by ventilation, and employees generally enter the dip coat area for short time periods (up to one hour). Vapors could leak into the dip coat and drying areas if the ventilation system is not running at peak efficiency. Odors in this area are often unpleasant even at the levels maintained by the ventilation system. While _____ notes that respiratory protection is not required in this area, the company recognizes employee concern about breathing vapors and about having to work in an unpleasant environment. Accordingly, employees may voluntarily choose to wear a half facepiece APR with organic vapor cartridges when working in this area.

- Assembly: Ventilation controls on sanders are in place, but employees continue to be exposed to respirable wood dust at 2.5 - 6.0 mg/m^3 (8-hour TWA); half facepiece APRs with P100 filters and goggles are required for employees sanding wood pieces in the assembly department. PAPRs will be available for employees who are unable to wear an APR. The planned substitution for aqueous-based glues will eliminate exposures to formaldehyde, methylene chloride, and epoxy resins. Until then, appropriate respiratory protec-

tion is required according to the Formaldehyde and Methylene Chloride standards, and the cartridge, filter, and canister requirements of the Respiratory Protection standard at *paragraph (d)(3)(ii)*.

- Maintenance: Because of potential IDLH conditions, employees cleaning dip coat tanks must wear a pressure demand SAR during the performance of this task. Employees may voluntarily wear half facepiece APRs with P100 cartridges when cleaning spray booth walls or changing booth filters, and half facepiece APRs with organic vapor cartridges when loading coating agents into supply systems. Although exposure monitoring has shown that exposures are kept within PELs during these procedures, _____ will provide respirators to workers who are concerned about potential exposures.

OSHA®
Occupational Safety and
Health Administration

Table 2: Hazard Assessment (Sample Program) - Date of Assessment

Department	Contaminants	Exposure Level (8-hr TWA)	PEL	Controls
Spray Booth Cleaning Area	Possible emergency spills of hazardous substances			Alarms; escape respirators located in Locker #1 in Spray Booth
Dip Coat/ Drying Area	Potentially malfunctioning ventilation system; leak in supply			Alarms; escape respirators located in Storage Area #3 in the Dip Coat/Drying Area
Coatings Storage Area	Leaks/spills			Alarms; escape respirators located in locker #4 in the Coating Storage Area
Dip Coat Tank Cleaner	Possible IDLH		IDLH	Pressure demand SAR; confined space entry procedures as specified in the Confined Space Program for this workplace
Preparation Coat/Assembly Area/Maintenance	Respirable wood dust, other particulates, vapors; can be IDLH		Can be IDLH	Pressure demand SAR
Preparation Sanding	Respirable wood dust	2.5 - 7.0 mg/m³	15 mg/m³	Half facepiece APRs with P100 filters and goggles
Preparation cleaning/clean and strip	Methylene Chloride	70 ppm	25 ppm PEL 12.5 ppm AL 125 ppm STEL	Awaiting the installation of ventilation; until then, SAR hood with continuous flow
Coat/Spray Booth				At Program Administrator's discretion: SAR Hood with continuous flow
Coat Spray/Cleaning Spray Gun				When cleaning spray guns **only**, employees may opt for APRs with organic vapor cartridges
Coating/Dip Tank/Drying				Ventilation; employees work in this area for short periods of time only (an hour); due to the presence of smells and vapors, employees may voluntarily choose to wear half mask APRs with organic vapor filters
Assembly	Respirable wood dust	2.5 - 6.0 mg/m³ IDLH	15 mg/m³	Although ventilation has been provided, employees still experience respirable dust; half facepiece APRs with P100 filters and goggles; PAPRs can be made available to workers who cannot wear half mask APRs; substitution of aqueous-based glues will eliminate exposures to formaldehyde, methylene chloride, and epoxy resins
Maintenance: cleaning dip coat tanks				Pressure demand SAR while performing this task

Updating the Hazard Assessment – The Program Administrator:

- Must revise and update the hazard assessment as needed (i.e., any time work process changes may potentially affect exposure). If an employee feels that respiratory protection is needed during a particular activity, he/she is to contact his or her supervisor or the **Program Administrator**. The Program Administrator then:

- Will evaluate the potential hazard, arranging for outside assistance as necessary.

- Will then communicate the results of that assessment back to the employees. If it is determined that respiratory protection is necessary, all other elements of this program will be in effect for those tasks, and this program will be updated accordingly.

- Will ensure that all respirators are certified by the National Institute for Occupational Safety and Health (NIOSH) and are used in accord with the terms of that certification.

- Will also ensure that all filters, cartridges, and canisters must be labeled with the appropriate NIOSH certification label. The label must not be removed or defaced while it is in use.

- Regarding **Voluntary Respirator Use**, the following statement is needed: _____ will provide respirators at no charge to employees for voluntary use for the following work processes/areas:

  Employees may wear half facepiece APRs with organic vapor cartridges while working in the dip coat area.

  Warehouse workers may wear filtering facepieces.

  Spray Booth Operators may wear half facepiece APRs with organic vapor cartridges while cleaning spray guns.

  Maintenance personnel may wear half facepiece APRs with P100 cartridges while cleaning spray booth walls, and organic vapor cartridges while loading spray guns.

The Program Administrator will also:

- Provide all employees who voluntarily choose to wear either of the above respirators with a copy of *Appendix D* of the standard specified by the *Respiratory Protection standard (29 CFR 1910.134)*. (*Appendix D* details the requirements for voluntary use of respirators by workers.) Workers choosing to wear a half facepiece APR must comply with the procedures for medical evaluation, respirator use,

and cleaning, maintenance and storage.

- Authorize voluntary use of respiratory protective equipment as requested by all other workers on a case-by-case basis, depending on specific workplace conditions and the results of the medical evaluations. Voluntary use does not require compliance with these specific provisions of the standard.

Medical Evaluation: Employees who are either required to wear respirators, or who choose to wear an APR voluntarily, must pass a medical exam before being permitted to wear a respirator on the job. Employees are not permitted to wear respirators until a PLHCP has determined that they are medically able to do so. Any employee refusing the medical evaluation will not be allowed to work in an area requiring respirator use. A PLHCP _____, where all company medical services are provided, will provide the medical evaluations.

Medical evaluation procedures are as follows:

- The medical evaluation will be conducted using the questionnaire provided in *Appendix C* of the Respiratory Protection standard.

- The **Program Administrator** will provide a copy of this questionnaire to all employees requiring medical evaluations.

- To the extent feasible, the company will assist employees who are unable to read the questionnaire (by providing help in reading the questionnaire). When this is not possible, the employee will be sent directly to the physician for medical evaluation.

- All affected employees will be given a copy of the medical questionnaire to fill out, along with a stamped and addressed envelope for mailing the questionnaire to the company physician.

Employees will:

- Be permitted to fill out the questionnaire on company time.

- Be granted follow-up medical exams as required by the Respiratory Protection standard, and/or as deemed necessary by _____ the PLHCP.

- Be granted the opportunity to speak with the physician about their medical evaluation, if they so request.

The Program Administrator has provided _____ _____ the physician with:

Occupational Safety and Health Administration

- A copy of this program, and a copy of the Respiratory Protection standard.
- The list of hazardous substances by work area, and for each employee requiring evaluation, his or her work area or job.
- The employee's title, proposed respirator type and weight, length of time required to wear the respirator, expected physical work load (light, moderate, or heavy), potential temperature and humidity extremes, and any additional protective clothing required.

Any employee required for medical reasons to wear a positive pressure air purifying respirator will be provided with a powered air purifying respirator.

After an employee has received clearance and begun to wear his or her respirator, additional medical evaluations will be provided if:

- The employee reports signs and/or symptoms related to their ability to use a respirator, such as shortness of breath, dizziness, chest pains, or wheezing.
- The PLHCP _____ or supervisor informs the **Program Administrator** that the employee needs to be reevaluated, additional medical evaluation will be provided.
- Information from this program, including observations made during fit testing and program evaluation, indicates a need for reevaluation.
- An example of the PLHCP's or the supervisor's observations that additional medical evaluation is needed could be that there has been a change in workplace conditions that may result in an increased physiological burden on the employee.

A list of _____ employees currently included in medical surveillance is provided in Table 3 of this program. All examinations and questionnaires are to remain confidential between the employee and the physician.

Fit Testing:

- Fit testing is required for employees wearing half facepiece APRs for exposure to wood dust in Prep and Assembly, and maintenance workers who wear a tight-fitting SAR for dip tank cleaning.
- Employees voluntarily wearing half facepiece APRs may also be fit tested upon request.
- Employees who are required to wear half facepiece APRs will be fit tested:

  - Prior to being allowed to wear any respirator with a tight fitting facepiece.
  - Annually.
  - When there are changes in the employee's physical condition that could affect respiratory fit (e.g., obvious change in body weight, facial scarring, etc.).

- Employees will be fit tested with the make, model, and size of respirator that they will actually wear.
- Employees will be provided with several models and sizes of respirators so that they may find an optimal fit.
- Fit testing of PAPRs is to be conducted in the negative pressure mode. The **Program Administrator** will conduct fit tests following the OSHA approved Bitrex Solution Aerosol QLFT Protocol in *Appendix A of the Respiratory Protection standard*. The **Program Administrator** has determined that QNFT is not required for the respirators used under current conditions at _____. If conditions affecting respirator use change, the **Program Administrator** will evaluate on a case-by-case basis whether QNFT is required.

Respirator Use - Responsibilities for **Employees** are that they:

- Will use their respirators under conditions specified by this program, and in accord with the training they receive on the use of each particular model. In addition, the respirator must not be used in a manner for which it is not certified by NIOSH or by its manufacturer.
- Must conduct user seal checks each time that they wear their respirator.
- Must use either the positive or negative pressure check (depending on which test works best for them) specified in *Appendix B-1 of the Respiratory Protection standard*.
- Must leave the work area to go to the locker room to maintain their respirator for the following reasons:

  - to clean their respirator if the respirator is impeding their ability to work;
  - to change filters or cartridges, or replace parts; or
  - to inspect the respirator if it stops functioning as intended.

- Should notify their supervisor before leaving the area.
- Not wear tight-fitting respirators if they have any condition, such as facial scars, facial hair, or missing dentures, that prevents them from achieving a good seal.

- Not wear headphones, jewelry, or other articles that may interfere with the facepiece-to-face seal.

Emergency Procedures:

- The following work areas have been identified as having foreseeable emergencies:

  - Spray Booth Cleaning Area - spill of hazardous waste

  - Dip Coat Area - malfunction of ventilation system, leak in supply system

  - Coatings Storage Area - spill or leak of hazardous substances

- When the alarm sounds, employees in the affected department must immediately don their emergency escape respirator, shut down their process equipment, and exit the work area.

- All other employees must immediately evacuate the building. _____'s Emergency Action Plan describes these procedures (including proper evacuation routes and rally points) in greater detail.

- Emergency escape respirators are located in:

  - Locker #1 in the Spray Booth Area

  - Storage cabinet #3 in the Dip Coat/Drying Area

  - Locker #4 in the Coatings Storage Area

- Respiratory protection in these instances is for escape purposes only. _____ employees are not trained as emergency responders, and are not authorized to act in such a manner.

Respirator Malfunction

1. APR Respirator Malfunction:

- For any malfunction of an APR (e.g., breakthrough, facepiece leakage, or improperly working valve), the respirator wearer must inform his or her supervisor that the respirator no longer functions, and go to the designated safe area to maintain the respirator. The supervisor must ensure that the employee receives the needed parts to repair the respirator, or is provided with a new respirator.

2. Atmosphere-Supplying Respirator Malfunction:

- All workers wearing atmosphere-supplying respirators will work with a buddy.

- Buddies should assist workers who experience an SAR malfunction as follows:

  - If a worker in the spray booth experiences a malfunction of an SAR, he or she should signal to the buddy that he or she has had a respirator malfunction. The buddy shall don an emergency escape respirator and aid the worker in immediately exiting the spray booth.

  - Workers cleaning wood pieces or assembled furniture in the Prep department will work with a buddy. If one of the workers experiences a respirator malfunction, he/she shall signal this to their buddy. The buddy must immediately stop what he or she is doing to escort the worker to the Prep staging area where the worker can safely remove the SAR.

IDLH Procedures

- The **Program Administrator** has identified the following area as presenting the potential for IDLH conditions:

- **Dip Coat Tank Cleaning:**

  - Maintenance workers will be periodically required to enter the dip tank to perform scheduled or unscheduled maintenance.

  - In such cases, workers will follow the permit-required confined space entry procedures specified in the _____ Confined Space Program.

  - As specified above, the **Program Administrator** has determined that workers entering this area must wear a pressure demand SAR.

  - In addition, an appropriately trained and equipped standby person must remain outside the dip tank and maintain constant voice and visual communication with the worker.

  - In the event of an emergency requiring the standby person to enter the IDLH environment, the standby person must immediately notify the **Program Administrator** and will proceed with rescue operations in accord with rescue procedures outlined in the _____ Confined Space Program.

Air Quality

- For supplied-air respirators, only Grade D breathing air is to be used in the cylinders.

- The **Program Administrator** will coordinate deliveries of compressed air with the company's vendor, Compressed Air Inc., and require Compressed Air Inc. to certify that the air in the cylinders meets the specifications of Grade D breathing air.

- The **Program Administrator** will maintain a minimum air supply of one fully charged replacement

cylinder for each SAR unit. In addition, cylinders may be recharged as necessary from the breathing air cascade system located near the respirator storage area.

- The air for this system is provided by _____'s supplier, and deliveries of new air are coordinated by the **Program Administrator**.

Cleaning, Maintenance and Change Schedules and Storage

Cleaning

- Respirators are to be regularly cleaned and disinfected at the designated respirator cleaning station located in the employee locker room.

- Respirators issued for the exclusive use of a employee are to be cleaned as often as necessary, but at least once a day for workers in the Prep and Assembly departments.

- Atmosphere-supplying and emergency use respirators are to be cleaned and disinfected after each use.

- The following procedure is to be used when cleaning and disinfecting respirators:

  - Disassemble respirator, removing any filters, canisters, or cartridges.

  - Wash the facepiece and associated parts in a mild detergent with warm water. Do not use organic solvents.

  - Rinse completely in clean warm water.

  - Wipe the respirator with disinfectant wipes (70% Isopropyl Alcohol) to kill germs.

  - Air dry in a clean area.

  - Reassemble the respirator and replace any defective parts.

  - Place in a clean, dry plastic bag or other airtight container.

- Note: The **Program Administrator** will ensure an adequate supply of appropriate cleaning and disinfection material at the cleaning station. If supplies are low, employees should contact their supervisor, who will inform the **Program Administrator**.

Maintenance

- Respirators are to be properly maintained at all times to ensure that they function properly and adequately protect the employee.

- Maintenance involves a thorough visual inspection for cleanliness and defects.

- Worn or deteriorated parts will be replaced prior to use.

- No components will be replaced or repairs made beyond those recommended by the manufacturer.

- Repairs to regulators or alarms of atmosphere-supplying respirators will be conducted by the manufacturer.

- The following checklist will be used when inspecting respirators:

  - Facepiece:
    - cracks, tears, or holes
    - facemask distortion
    - cracked or loose lenses/faceshield

  - Valves:
    - Residue or dirt
    - Cracks or tears in valve material

  - Headstraps:
    - breaks or tears
    - broken buckles

  - Filters/Cartridges:
    - approval designation
    - gaskets
    - cracks or dents in housing
    - proper cartridge for hazard

  - Air Supply Systems:
    - breathing air quality/grade
    - condition of supply hoses
    - hose connections
    - settings on regulators and valves

- Employees are permitted to leave their work area and go to a designated area that is free of respiratory hazards when they need to wash their face and respirator facepiece to prevent any eye or skin irritation, or to replace the filter, cartridge or canister, or when they detect vapor or gas breakthrough or leakage in the facepiece or detect any other damage to the respirator or its components.

Change Schedules

- Employees wearing APRs or PAPRs with P100 filters for protection against wood dust and other particulates need to change the cartridges on their respirators when they first begin to experience difficulty breathing (i.e., resistance) while wearing their masks.

- Based on discussions with our respirator distributor about _____'s workplace exposure conditions, employees voluntarily wearing APRs with organic vapor cartridges must change the cartridges on their respirators at the end of each work week to ensure the continued effectiveness of the respirators.

Storage

- Respirators must be stored in a clean, dry area, and in accord with the manufacturer's recommendations.

- Each employee will clean and inspect their own air-purifying respirator in accord with the provisions of this program, and will store their respirator in a plastic bag in their own locker.

- Each employee will have his/her name on the bag, and that bag will only be used to store that employee's respirator.

- Atmosphere-supplying respirators will be stored in the storage cabinet outside of the **Program Administrator's** office.

- The **Program Administrator** will store _____'s supply of respirators and respirator components in their original manufacturer's packaging in the equipment storage room.

Defective Respirators

- Respirators that are defective or have defective parts must be taken out of service immediately.

- If, during an inspection, an employee discovers a defect in a respirator, he/she is to bring the defect to the attention of his or her supervisor.

- Supervisors will give all defective respirators to the **Program Administrator**.

- The **Program Administrator** will decide whether to:

  - Temporarily take the respirator out of service until it can be repaired.

  - Perform a simple fix on the spot such as replacing a headstrap.

  - Dispose of the respirator due to an irreparable problem or defect.

- When a respirator is taken out of service, the respirator will be tagged out of service, and the employee will be given a replacement of the same make, model and size.

- If the employee is not given a replacement of the same make, model and size, then the employee must be fit tested.

- All tagged out-of-service respirators will be kept in the storage cabinet inside the **Program Administrator's** office.

Training

- The **Program Administrator** will provide training to respirator users and their supervisors on the contents of the _____ Respiratory Protection Program and their responsibilities under it, and on the OSHA Respiratory Protection standard.

- Workers will be trained prior to using a respirator in the workplace.

- The training must be comprehensive, understandable and recur annually, and more often if necessary.

- As with any employee, supervisors must be trained prior to using a respirator in the workplace; they also should be trained prior to supervising workers who must wear respirators if the supervisors themselves do not use a respirator.

- Supervisors will provide the basic information on respirators in Appendix D of the Respiratory Protection standard to employees who wear respirators when not required by the employer to do so.

- Supervisors will ensure that each employee can demonstrate knowledge of at least the following:

  Why the respirator is necessary and how improper fit, usage, or maintenance can compromise the protective effect of the respirator;

  What the limitations and capabilities of the respirator are;

  How to use the respirator effectively in emergency situations, including situations in which the respirator malfunctions;

  How to inspect, put on and remove, use, and check the seals of the respirator;

  What the procedures are for maintenance and storage of the respirator;

  How to recognize medical signs and symptoms that may limit or prevent the effective use of respirators; and

  The general requirements of the Respiratory Protection standard.

- Supervisors will ensure that employees will be retrained annually or as needed (e.g., if they change departments and need to use a different respirator).

  An employer who is able to demonstrate that a new employee has received training within the last 12 months that addresses the elements specified in

paragraph (k)(1)(i) through (vii) is not required to repeat such training provided that, as required by *paragraph (k)(1)*, the employee can demonstrate knowledge of those element(s).

Previous training not repeated initially by the employer must be provided no later than 12 months from the date of the previous training.

Retraining shall be administered annually, and when the following situations occur:

Changes in the workplace or the type of respirator render previous training obsolete;

Inadequacies in the employee's knowledge or use of the respirator indicate that the worker has not retained the requisite understanding or skill; or

Any other situation arises in which retraining appears necessary to ensure safe respirator use.

The basic advisory information on respirators, as presented in Appendix D of the Respiratory Protection standard, shall be provided by the employer in any written or oral format to employees who wear respirators when such use is not required by this section or by the employer.

5. Program Evaluation

- The **Program Administrator** will conduct periodic evaluations of the workplace to ensure that the provisions of this program are being implemented.

- The evaluations will include regular consultations with employees who use respirators and their supervisors, site inspections, air monitoring and a review of records.

- List factors to be evaluated *(see (l)(2).)*

- Problems identified will be noted in an inspection log and corrected by the **Program Administrator**.

- These findings will be reported to _____ management, and the report will list plans to correct deficiencies in the respirator program and target dates for implementing those corrections.

6. Documentation and Recordkeeping

- A written copy of this program and the OSHA standard is kept in the **Program Administrator's** office and is available to all employees who wish to review it.

- Also maintained in the **Program Administrator's** office are copies of training materials.

- Copies of fit test records *(see (m)(2) of the standard)*. These records will be updated as new fit tests are conducted.

- These records will be updated as new employees are trained and as existing employees receive refresher training.

- The **Program Administrator** will also maintain copies of the records for all employees covered under the respirator program (except medical records).

- The completed medical questionnaire and the PLHCP's documented findings are confidential and will remain at _____. The company will only retain the physician's written recommendation regarding each employee's ability to wear a respirator.

Table 3: A list of _____ employees currently included in the medical surveillance program. Date of Listing.

Name of first employee _____	Date_____
Second name _____	Date_____
Next name_____	Date_____
Next name_____	Date_____
Next name_____	Date_____
Next name_____	Date_____
Next name_____	Date_____
Next name_____	Date_____
Last name_____	Date_____

Attachment 5:
NIOSH MultiVapor Information

The National Institute for Occupational Safety and Health (NIOSH) announced new computer software that enables administrators of workplace respiratory protection programs to consider the effects of relative humidity on the service life of NIOSH-approved organic vapor (OV) chemical cartridges. This software assists program administrators, in workplaces where air-purifying respirators are used, in reducing on-the-job respiratory exposures to potentially harmful organic vapors from a single volatile source, such as an individual paint, thinner, or solvent.

The ambient relative humidity in the environment in which an air-purifying respirator is used or stored is one of the factors that, over time, can cause the sorbent in a cartridge to lose its ability to collect organic vapors from the air breathed in through the cartridge. Collecting the vapors removes them from the air that the respirator user breathes into his or her body. Advances in computational capabilities of personal computers, and verification of the mathematical model through recent research, made possible the addition of this critical factor to the software program that was not included in previous government versions.

The new software program also incorporates factors that were used in previous computer software available from the government. Those factors include, for example, the type of air contaminant against which the chemical cartridge will protect the user, the concentration of the contaminant, the parameters of the cartridge and the rate at which the user is working.

By using the software, a respirator program administrator can determine when the cartridge is likely to reach the end of its service life or effectiveness; this is the point at which "breakthrough" is likely to occur as the sorbent no longer is able to collect organic vapors at the needed capacity. With that information, the administrator will know when to schedule a replacement of the cartridge.

"Especially in situations when the use of air-purifying respirators may be necessary for hours, knowing when to change the organic vapor cartridge is critical for keeping the user safe and healthy," said NIOSH Director John Howard, M.D. "By adding in a key factor that was not included in previous government software, program administrators can feel more confident in the schedules they set for changing cartridges."

The new computer software reflects the concept of government leadership through collaboration with diverse technical organizations. The software resulted from research conducted by Los Alamos National Laboratory (LANL), in conjunction with a partnership by NIOSH, LANL, the Occupational Safety and Health Administration (OSHA), the International Safety Equipment Association (ISEA), the American Chemistry Council (ACC), the Synthetic Organic Chemical Manufacturers Association (SOCMA), the National Paint and Coatings Association (NPCA), and the American Petroleum Institute (API), organized and led by ORC Worldwide. The consortium provided funding for the initial research and then joined with NIOSH, which provided funding necessary to complete the work.

The NIOSH website for calculating end of service indicators for organics, called "MultiVapor," can be accessed at: *http://www.cdc.gov/niosh/npptl/multivapor/multivapor.html*.

OSHA®
Occupational Safety and
Health Administration

Attachment 6:
NIOSH Tables of Cartridges and Canisters by APFs (Modified to OSHA APFs)

Table 1: Particulate Respirators

Assigned protection[1] factor	Type of Respirator
5	Quarter mask respirator
10	Any air-purifying elastomeric half mask respirator equipped with appropriate type of particulate filter.[2]
	Appropriate filtering facepiece respirator.[2,3]
	Any air-purifying full facepiece respirator equipped with appropriate type of particulate filter.[2]
	Any negative pressure (demand) supplied-air respirator equipped with a half mask.
25	Any powered air-purifying respirator equipped with a loose-fitting hood or helmet and a high efficiency (HEPA) filter.
	Any continuous flow supplied-air respirator equipped with a hood or helmet.
50	Any air-purifying full facepiece respirator equipped with N-100, R-100, or P-100 filter(s).[4]
	Any powered air-purifying respirator equipped with a tight-fitting facepiece (half or full facepiece) and a high-efficiency filter.
	Any negative pressure (demand) supplied-air respirator equipped with a full facepiece.
	Any continuous flow supplied-air respirator equipped with a tight-fitting facepiece (half or full facepiece).
	Any negative pressure (pressure demand) self-contained respirator equipped with a half or full facepiece.
1,000	Any pressure-demand, or other positive pressure mode, supplied-air respirator equipped with a full facepiece
	Any powered air-purifying respirator with helmet or hood for which the employer has provided evidence provided by the respirator manufacturer that testing of these respirators demonstrates performance at a level of protection of 1,000 or greater.
10,000	Any pressure-demand, or other positive pressure mode self-contained respirator equipped with a full facepiece.
	Any pressure-demand self contained breathing apparatus respirator equipped with a full facepiece helmet or hood.

[1] The protection offered by a given respirator is contingent upon (1) the respirator user adhering to complete program requirements (such as the ones required by OSHA in 29 CFR 1910.134), (2) the use of NIOSH-certified respirators in their approved configuration, and (3) individual fit testing to rule out those respirators that cannot achieve a good fit on individual workers.

[2] "Appropriate" means that the filter medium will provide protection against the particulate in question. See step 4.0 for information on the presence or absence of oil particulates.

[3] An APF of 10 can only be achieved if the respirator is qualitatively or quantitatively fit tested on individual workers.

[4] N, P, and R series: Since 1995, NIOSH has been approving three series of particle-filtering respirators, designated N, R and P. Within each series, three levels of efficiency in removing the laboratory test aerosols are certified: 95%, 99% and 99.97%. N-series filters are not required to demonstrate resistance to the potentially "degrading" effects of oils, and are, therefore, not intended for use in workplace atmospheres that contain oily aerosols. In this context, "degrading" means that exposure to an agent may cause an increase in filter penetration measured under laboratory test conditions. R and P series filters must demonstrate oil resistance when tested with dioctyl phthalate (DOP), which is described as a "highly degrading" oil aerosol. As a result both R and P filters can be used in workplace atmospheres that contain oily aerosols, as well as those that do not. In other cases, NIOSH-certified electret filters are necessary since the filtering efficiency of respiratory protection may be degraded by electrical charges. Electret filters consist of electrically charged fibers, such as polymer fibers, and they are widely used in particulate respirators. The charges enhance their filtration efficiency, particularly for submicrometer aerosols, without a corresponding increase in pressure drop across the filter. Electret filters can be N, P, R filters across all of the filtering efficiencies of 95% through 99.97%.

Table 2: Gas/Vapor Respirators

Assigned protection[1] factor	Type of Respirator
10	Any air-purifying half mask respirator equipped with appropriate gas/vapor cartridges.[2]
	Any negative pressure (demand) supplied-air respirator equipped with a half mask.
25	Any powered air-purifying respirator with a loose-fitting hood or helmet equipped with appropriate gas/vapor cartridges.[2]
	Any continuous flow supplied-air respirator equipped with a hood or helmet.
50	Any air-purifying full facepiece respirator equipped with appropriate gas/vapor cartridges[2] or gas mask (canister respirator).[2]
	Any powered air-purifying respirator equipped with a tight-fitting facepiece (half facepiece) and appropriate gas/vapor cartridges or canisters.[2]
	Any negative pressure (demand) supplied-air respirator equipped with a full facepiece.
	Any continuous flow supplied-air respirator equipped with a tight-fitting facepiece (half facepiece).
	Any negative pressure (pressure demand) self-contained respirator equipped with a half facepiece.
1,000	Any pressure-demand supplied-air respirator equipped with a half or full facepiece.
10,000	Any pressure-demand self-contained respirator equipped with a full facepiece.
	Any pressure-demand supplied-air respirator equipped with a full facepiece in combination with an auxiliary pressure-demand self-contained breathing apparatus.

[1] The protection offered by a given respirator is contingent upon (1) the respirator user adhering to complete program requirements (such as the ones required by OSHA in 29 CFR 1910.134), (2) the use of NIOSH-certified respirators in their approved configuration, and (3) individual fit testing to rule out those respirators that cannot achieve a good fit on individual workers.

[2] Select a cartridge/canister certified to be used for the specific class of chemicals or the specific gas/vapor found in your workplace.

OSHA®
Occupational Safety and
Health Administration

Table 3: Combination Gas/Vapor and Particulate Respirators

Assigned protection[1] factor	Type of Respirator
10	Any air-purifying half mask respirator equipped with appropriate gas/vapor cartridges[2] in combination with appropriate type of particulate filter.[3]
	Any full facepiece respirator with appropriate gas/vapor cartridges[2] in combination with appropriate type of particulate filter.[3]
	Any negative pressure (demand) supplied-air respirator equipped with a half mask.
25	Any powered air-purifying respirator with a loose-fitting hood or helmet that is equipped with an appropriate gas/vapor cartridge[2] in combination with a high-efficiency particulate filter.
	Any continuous flow supplied-air respirator equipped with a hood or helmet.
50	Any air-purifying full facepiece respirator equipped with appropriate gas/vapor cartridges[2] in combination with an N-100, R-100 or P-100 filter or an appropriate canister[2] incorporating an N-100, P-100 or R-100 filter.
	Any powered air-purifying respirator with a tight-fitting facepiece (half or full facepiece) equipped with appropriate gas/vapor cartridges[2] in combination with a high-efficiency filter or an appropriate canister[2] incorporating a high-efficiency filter.
	Any negative pressure (demand) supplied-air respirator equipped with a full facepiece.
	Any continuous flow supplied-air respirator equipped with a tight-fitting facepiece (half or full facepiece).
	Any negative pressure (demand) self-contained respirator equipped with a full facepiece.
1,000	Any pressure-demand supplied-air respirator equipped with a half or full mask.
10,000	Any pressure-demand self-contained respirator equipped with a full facepiece.
	Any pressure-demand supplied-air respirator equipped with a full facepiece in combination with an auxiliary pressure-demand self-contained breathing apparatus.

[1] The protection offered by a given respirator is contingent upon (1) the respirator user adhering to complete program requirements (such as the ones required by OSHA in 29 CFR 1910.134), (2) the use of NIOSH-certified respirators in their approved configuration, and (3) individual fit testing to rule out those respirators that cannot achieve a good fit on individual workers.

[2] Select a cartridge/canister certified to be used for the specific class of chemicals or the specific gas/vapor found in your workplace.

[3] "Appropriate" means that the filter medium will provide protection against the particulate in question.

NIOSH publication 2005-100, Respirator Selection.

Complaints, Emergencies and Further Assistance

Workers have the right to a safe workplace. The *Occupational Safety and Health Act of 1970* (OSH Act) was passed to prevent workers from being killed or seriously harmed at work. The law requires employers to provide their employees with working conditions that are free of known dangers. Workers may file a complaint to have OSHA inspect their workplace if they believe that their employer is not following OSHA standards or that there are serious hazards. Further, the Act gives complainants the right to request that their names not be revealed to their employers. It is also against the law for an employer to fire, demote, transfer, or discriminate in any way against a worker for filing a complaint or using other OSHA rights.

To report an emergency, file a complaint, or seek OSHA advice, assistance, or products, call (800) 321-OSHA (6742) or contact your nearest OSHA regional, area, or state plan office listed or linked to at the end of this publication. The teletypewriter (TTY) number is (877) 889-5627. You can also file a complaint online by visiting OSHA's website at www.osha.gov. Most complaints submitted online may be resolved informally over the phone or by fax with your employer. Written complaints, that are signed by a worker or their representative and submitted to the closest OSHA office, are more likely to result in an on-site OSHA inspection.

Compliance Assistance Resources

OSHA can provide extensive help through a variety of programs, including free workplace consultations, compliance assistance, voluntary protection programs, strategic partnerships, alliances, and training and education. For more information on any of the programs listed below, visit OSHA's website at www.osha.gov or call 1-800-321-OSHA (6742).

Establishing an Injury and Illness Prevention Program

The key to a safe and healthful work environment is a comprehensive injury and illness prevention program.

Injury and illness prevention programs, known by a variety of names, are universal interventions that can substantially reduce the number and severity of workplace injuries and alleviate the associated financial burdens on U.S. workplaces. Many states have requirements or voluntary guidelines for workplace injury and illness prevention programs. In addition, numerous employers in the United States already manage safety using injury and illness prevention programs, and we believe that all employers can and should do the same. Employers in the construction industry are already required to have a health and safety program. Most successful injury and illness prevention programs are based on a common set of key elements. These include management leadership, worker participation, hazard identification, hazard prevention and control, education and training, and program evaluation and improvement. Visit OSHA's website at http://www.osha.gov/dsg/topics/safetyhealth/index.html for more information and guidance on establishing effective injury and illness prevention programs in the workplace.

Compliance Assistance Specialists

OSHA has compliance assistance specialists throughout the nation who can provide information to employers and workers about OSHA standards, short educational programs on specific hazards or OSHA rights and responsibilities, and information on additional compliance assistance resources. Contact your local OSHA office for more information.

OSHA Consultation Service for Small Employers

The OSHA Consultation Service provides **free assistance** to small employers to help them identify and correct hazards, and to improve their injury and illness prevention programs. Most of these services are delivered on site by state government agencies or universities using well-trained professional staff.

Consultation services are available to private sector employers. Priority is given to small employers with the most hazardous operations or in the most high-hazard industries. These programs are largely funded by OSHA and are delivered at no cost to employers who request help. Consultation services are separate from enforcement activities. To request such services, an employer can phone or write to the OSHA Consultation Program. See the Small Business section of OSHA's website for contact information for the consultation offices in every state.

- ### Safety and Health Achievement Recognition Program
  Under the consultation program, certain exemplary employers may request participation in OSHA's Safety and Health Achievement

Recognition Program (SHARP). Eligibility for participation includes, but is not limited to, receiving a full-service, comprehensive consultation visit, correcting all identified hazards, and developing an effective injury and illness prevention program.

Cooperative Programs

OSHA offers cooperative programs to help prevent fatalities, injuries and illnesses in the workplace.

- **OSHA's Alliance Program**

  Through the Alliance Program, OSHA works with groups committed to worker safety and health to prevent workplace fatalities, injuries, and illnesses. These groups include businesses, trade or professional organizations, unions, consulates, faith- and community-based organizations, and educational institutions. OSHA and the groups work together to develop compliance assistance tools and resources, share information with workers and employers, and educate workers and employers about their rights and responsibilities.

- **Challenge Program**

  This program helps employers and workers improve their injury and illness prevention programs and implement an effective system to prevent fatalities, injuries and illnesses.

- **OSHA Strategic Partnership Program (OSPP)**

  Partnerships are formalized through tailored agreements designed to encourage, assist and recognize partner efforts to eliminate serious hazards and achieve model workplace safety and health practices.

- **Voluntary Protection Programs (VPP)**

  The VPP recognize employers and workers in private industry and federal agencies who have implemented effective injury and illness prevention programs and maintain injury and illness rates below national Bureau of Labor Statistics averages for their respective industries. In VPP, management, labor, and OSHA work cooperatively and proactively to prevent fatalities, injuries, and illnesses.

OSHA Training Institute Education Centers

The OSHA Training Institute (OTI) Education Centers are a national network of nonprofit organizations authorized by OSHA to conduct occupational safety and health training to private sector workers, supervisors and employers.

Susan Harwood Training and Education Grants

OSHA provides grants to nonprofit organizations to provide worker education and training on serious job hazards and avoidance/prevention strategies.

Information and Publications

OSHA has a variety of educational materials and electronic tools available on its website at www.osha.gov. These include Safety and Health Topics Pages, Safety Fact Sheets, Expert Advisor software, copies of regulations and compliance directives, videos and other information for employers and workers. OSHA's software programs and eTools walk you through safety and health issues and common problems to find the best solutions for your workplace.

OSHA's extensive publications help explain OSHA standards, job hazards, and mitigation strategies and provide assistance in developing effective injury and illness prevention programs.

For a listing of free publications, visit OSHA's website at www.osha.gov or call 1-800-321-OSHA (6742).

QuickTakes

OSHA's free, twice-monthly online newsletter, *QuickTakes*, offers the latest news about OSHA initiatives and products to assist employers and workers in finding and preventing workplace hazards. To sign up for *QuickTakes*, visit OSHA's website at www.osha.gov and click on *QuickTakes* at the top of the page.

Contacting OSHA

To order additional copies of this publication, to get a list of other OSHA publications, to ask questions or to get more information, to contact OSHA's free consultation service, or to file a confidential complaint, contact OSHA at 1-800-321-OSHA (6742), (TTY) 1-877-889-5627 or visit www.osha.gov.

**For assistance, contact us.
We are OSHA. We can help.
It's confidential.**

OSHA Regional Offices

Region I
Boston Regional Office
(CT*, ME, MA, NH, RI, VT*)
JFK Federal Building, Room E340
Boston, MA 02203
(617) 565-9860 (617) 565-9827 Fax

Region II
New York Regional Office
(NJ*, NY*, PR*, VI*)
201 Varick Street, Room 670
New York, NY 10014
(212) 337-2378 (212) 337-2371 Fax

Region III
Philadelphia Regional Office
(DE, DC, MD*, PA, VA*, WV)
The Curtis Center
170 S. Independence Mall West
Suite 740 West
Philadelphia, PA 19106-3309
(215) 861-4900 (215) 861-4904 Fax

Region IV
Atlanta Regional Office
(AL, FL, GA, KY*, MS, NC*, SC*, TN*)
61 Forsyth Street, SW, Room 6T50
Atlanta, GA 30303
(678) 237-0400 (678) 237-0447 Fax

Region V
Chicago Regional Office
(IL*, IN*, MI*, MN*, OH, WI)
230 South Dearborn Street
Room 3244
Chicago, IL 60604
(312) 353-2220 (312) 353-7774 Fax

Region VI
Dallas Regional Office
(AR, LA, NM*, OK, TX)
525 Griffin Street, Room 602
Dallas, TX 75202
(972) 850-4145 (972) 850-4149 Fax
(972) 850-4150 FSO Fax

Region VII
Kansas City Regional Office
(IA*, KS, MO, NE)
Two Pershing Square Building
2300 Main Street, Suite 1010
Kansas City, MO 64108-2416
(816) 283-8745 (816) 283-0547 Fax

Region VIII
Denver Regional Office
(CO, MT, ND, SD, UT*, WY*)
1999 Broadway, Suite 1690
Denver, CO 80202-5716
(720) 264-6550 (720) 264-6585 Fax

Region IX
San Francisco Regional Office
(AZ*, CA*, HI*, NV*, and American Samoa,
Guam and the Northern Mariana Islands)
90 7th Street, Suite 18100
San Francisco, CA 94103
(415) 625-2547 (415) 625-2534 Fax

Region X
Seattle Regional Office
(AK*, ID, OR*, WA*)
1111 Third Avenue, Suite 715
Seattle, WA 98101-3212
(206) 553-5930 (206) 553-6499 Fax

*These states and territories operate their own OSHA-approved job safety and health plans and cover state and local government employees as well as private sector employees. The Connecticut, Illinois, New Jersey, New York and Virgin Islands programs cover public employees only. (Private sector workers in these states are covered by Federal OSHA). States with approved programs must have standards that are identical to, or at least as effective as, the Federal OSHA standards.

Note: To get contact information for OSHA area offices, OSHA-approved state plan offices and OSHA consultation projects, please visit us online at www.osha.gov or call us at 1-800-321-OSHA (6742).

Occupational Safety and Health Administration

Notes

Notes

www.ingramcontent.com/pod-product-compliance
Lightning Source LLC
Chambersburg PA
CBHW081728170526
45167CB00009B/3739